Captured by Indians

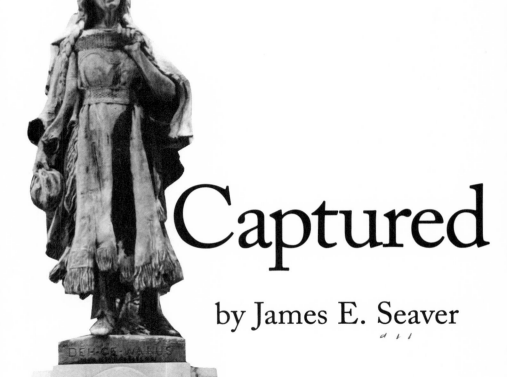

Captured

by James E. Seaver

The
Life of
Mary Jemison
by Indians

EDITED BY Karen Zeinert

LINNET BOOKS   1995

© 1995 by Karen Zeinert. All rights reserved.
First published 1995 by Linnet Books,
an imprint of The Shoe String Press, Inc.,
North Haven, Connecticut 06473.

Library of Congress Cataloging-in-Publication Data
Seaver, James E. (James Everett), 1787–1827.
[Narrative of the life of Mrs. Mary Jemison. Selections]
Captured by Indians: the life of Mary Jemison/
by James E. Seaver; edited by Karen Zeinert.   p.   cm.
Selections from A narrative of the life of Mrs. Mary Jemison, 1824.
Includes bibliographical references.
ISBN 0-208-02368-2 (alk. paper)
1. Jemison, Mary, 1743–1833—Juvenile literature.
2. Indian captivities—Genesee River Valley (Pa. and N.Y.)
—Juvenile literature.   3. Pioneers—Genesee River Valley
—Biography—Juvenile literature.   4. Genesee River Valley
—Biography—Juvenile literature.
[Jemison, Mary, 1743–1833.   2. Pioneers.   3. Indian captivities
—Genesee River Valley]   I. Title.
E99.S3J45725   1995   974.7′004975—dc20
[B]   95–6139   CIP   AC

The paper used in this publication meets the
minimum requirements of American National
Standard for Information Sciences—Permanence of
Paper for Printed Library Materials,
ANSI Z39.48-1984. ⊗

Book design by Abigail Johnston

Frontispiece photo: Statue of Mary Jemison.
Courtesy of Letchworth State Park, Castile,
New York

Printed in the United States of America

Contents

A Narrative of the Life of Mary Jemison
BY JAMES E. SEAVER

Background

When the first European settlers arrived in North America in the early 1600s, they found many Indian tribes living there. Most of the natives were willing to tolerate these newcomers, and some even taught the Europeans how to survive in the New World. But as the colonies grew and settlers pushed westward over the next 100 years, they turned forests into farms, destroying the natural habitat of deer and fur-bearing animals upon which the Indians depended for food, clothing, and pelts, which could be exchanged for necessities at fur-trading posts. In addition, Indian tribes had long before claimed the land now being settled by the colonists. Therefore, as white settlements grew in size and number upon the frontier, so did the Indians' anger. Eventually the Indians either had to move further westward—and into another Indian nation's territory—or fight for the land upon which they lived. Most chose to fight.

The Indians' anger toward white settlers, most of whom were British, was fanned by the French government in the early 1700s. French traders had established a booming fur trade with several tribes, especially those near the Great Lakes. More settlers meant fewer fur-bearing animals and, therefore, fewer pelts and less income for the traders.

In addition, the French government was afraid that if many English settlers moved into the area, the English would eventually claim it. So the French sought the help of the Indians to keep out the British, arguing that the British settlers, who meant to stay, were a serious threat to the Indians' way of life.

Egged on by the French, the Indians attacked white settlers. The warriors killed their victims, and following old Indian warfare customs, often tortured them before they died. Sometimes parts of the victims' bodies were cut off and eaten in front of them, or they were literally skinned alive.

Although whites blamed most atrocities on the Indians, the colonists participated in them as well. Colonial governments encouraged settlers to kill Indians by giving rewards. Most colonies offered $25 to $50—no small sum 250 years ago—for the scalp of a warrior, half of that for one belonging to a woman or child. No questions were asked about the killing, and the sites where scalps were redeemed stocked specially made scalping knives to make the gory task easier. In some instances, soldiers in colonial militias stalked Indians, shooting entire hunting parties when hunters stopped to rest and weapons had been put aside.

In 1754, the French and English—who along with other European powers were trying to write a peace treaty that would settle their long drawn-out war in Europe—

went to war in the New World over a number of issues, including territory on the frontier. The colonists called the war the "French and Indian War" because the French and the majority of the Indian tribes were allies against the English colonists. Although most tribes favored the French, many Iroquois could not bring themselves to support any cause in which their old enemies, the Huron Indians, were involved. Instead, the Iroquois who traded with the British supported England.

Loss of life among the Indians allied to the French was especially high during this war. As a result, warriors,

Stories about pioneers who were taken prisoner by Indians were popular for more than 100 years among white readers—much as adventure or crime stories are today. Courtesy of Dover Pictorial Archive Series.

following another old warfare custom, took white captives when they raided settlements. Although these captives could be turned in to the British for a reward, they were usually given or sold to Indian families who had lost warriors in battle, who then could do with them as they pleased.

Sometimes captives were tortured to death for revenge; more often, they were enslaved, and how these slaves were treated depended upon which family got them. In some cases, the prisoners were treated poorly and their lives were both insufferable and in constant peril. In other cases, the prisoners were taken by kind families that adopted them, and although they were not free to leave the tribe and had to follow orders, they were in many ways regarded as one of the family, that is, they had a fair share of food, clothing, shelter, and even respect and affection. However, other tribal members could make the life of a captive, adopted or not, very difficult, and even in the best of circumstances, no prisoner was ever really safe.

The practice of taking captives continued throughout the next conflict, the Revolutionary War. This time, most Indians backed the British because the English had tried to limit settlements on the land they won at the end of the French and Indian War. In addition, the British promised to stop development on the frontier if they won the war.

Regardless of when a prisoner was taken, the length of time he or she remained in captivity varied. Some were set free after a few years of labor; others were set free when a war ended. A few prisoners remained with their captors all their lives, by choice.

When freed, white captives were often encouraged by a curious public to publish their stories, and at least one hundred former prisoners did so. These stories, uniquely American, appealed to many people; in fact, everyone who liked to read about adventure, danger, and a struggle between heroes and villains. As a result, thousands of these "captivity narratives" were sold in North America, and later, as their popularity grew, thousands were sold in Europe as well.

Sometimes the stories were intended not just to entertain, but to make a point. For instance, some of the first stories pictured captives who survived as deeply religious people who drew upon their faith to get them through their ordeals. Writers and publishers hoped that such testimonials would encourage readers to examine—and strengthen—their own faith. More often, the stories portrayed Indians as "barbarians" and "demons," and their most controversial customs were emphasized. These stories were accepted as truth, and they were used for more than 100 years to justify killing Indians, seizing their land, and destroying their "inferior" and "ungodly" way of life.

One of the most popular captive stories was the narrative of Mary Jemison. Captured by Shawnees during the French and Indian War and given to the Senecas, a tribe that lived in what is now Ohio and western New York State, Mary chose to remain with the Indians when offered her freedom. Rumors about a white woman living with the Senecas circulated for many years among people living on the frontier. Her story—a narrative of a courageous woman who faced danger and adversity with grace and dignity—fascinated all who heard it. Eventually a publisher decided to print it. In 1823, he hired James Seaver, a local physician, to interview Mary. Seaver's book was published in 1824, and the first edition sold over *100,000* copies.

Mary's story is still popular for several reasons. It is one of the most complete narratives of a captive that we have from this era, covering events of more than seventy years. This gives us a better picture of what a captive's life could be like than a few isolated incidents would. Also, her story gives us insight into how the Indians really lived and how their lives changed over time. These were critical years of nation-building for a young country, and their effect upon Native Americans was telling. Mary's story also shows us how she changed and how she managed to survive in both worlds, the whites' and the Indians,' which was no small feat considering the trials she faced.

Editor's Note

The following narrative differs from James Seaver's in a number of ways. First, Dr. Seaver's opinions about the Indians and their culture have been cut from the narrative. Every attempt has been made to tell Mary's story as she told it, without comment. But readers should still be aware of the fact that Seaver asked the questions at the interview, and he was on a mission: his publisher was especially interested in printing stories of Indian atrocities, and at the very least, portraying the Senecas as "barbarians," a word that comes up often, even in this edited version. In addition, Seaver selected the material to be published. As a result, his effect on Mary's story is great.

Second, a biographical sketch of Mary's second husband, Hiokatoo, has been separated from Mary's narrative. She did not give the information Seaver published. Instead, it came from Mary's cousin, George Jemison, an interesting character, to the say the least. This sketch, like the illustrations and other materials I've added to make the text easier to understand, has been boxed-in to alert readers to the fact that the enclosed words are not Mary's.

Also, some incidents have been moved forward or backward in the text to provide better chronological order. The timeline that follows also will help readers keep events in order.

Wherever possible, the actual text of Mary's story has been used, and nineteenth century words, phrasing, and spelling have been kept to give readers a sense of the language at that time. Most words are easy to understand in their context. A few, though, are not, and the first time each one is used, it is italicized. This indicates that it is defined in the glossary. If words Mary used have very different meanings today, they were modernized to avoid confusion.

Several names have been changed. Seaver claimed that the Senecas called Mary "Dickewamis," a name that meant "a pretty girl or a pleasant, good thing." It is not clear where he got this name, and it is one that has been handed down in several stories. At least one historian claims that no such word as Dickewamis exists in the Seneca language, and he, along with many others, have used the name that appears in this text, "Dehgewanus," which means "two voices falling." Also, Seaver incorrectly identified the river to which Mary was taken as the Sciota River. Its correct name is the Scioto, and that name is used in this text. In Seaver's account, he broke Indian names into syllables the first time they appeared to make it easier for readers to pronounce them, and that practice was followed in this text.

One date is changed. Historians believe that Mary

was captured in 1758, not 1755 as she indicated in the original narrative, and 1758 is used in this text.

And finally, the preface and appendix that appeared in the original version were dropped. The appendix was gathered from many sources, not just interviews with Mary, and much of the information doesn't relate directly to Mary's story. It is her incredible life that is the focus of this book.

K.Z.

Timeline

This timeline puts in order some of the most important events in Mary Jemison's life, providing a framework for Mary's narrative.

1742 or 1743	Mary Jemison is born on board ship en route to America.
1756–1763	War between England and France, known as the French and Indian War in the colonies, takes place.
1758	Mary is captured by French and Shawnees and adopted by two Seneca women.
1760	Mary marries Sheninjee, a Delaware Indian.
1761	Mary's first child is born and dies.
1762	Thomas (second child) is born. Mary moves from Wiishto [Ohio] to Genishau [New York]. Sheninjee dies.

1766	Mary marries Hiokatoo, a Seneca Indian.
	John (third child) is born.
1773	Nancy (fourth child) is born.
1775–1781	American Revolution takes place.
	Four of the Six Iroquois Nations, including the Senecas, decide to support the British in the war.
1777	Betsey (fifth child) is born.
1778	Polly (sixth child) is born.
1779	General John Sullivan leads Continental Army soldiers in raids against four Iroquois nations loyal to England, including the Senecas.
1782	Jane (seventh child) is born.
1783	England and the U.S. ratify the Treaty of Paris, officially ending the Revolutionary War.
1784	Congress announces that the four Iroquois nations that supported the British are to be considered conquered people.
	Jesse (eighth child) is born.
1793 or 1794	Jane dies.
1797	Mary attends the Council at Big Tree to receive her land from the Senecas.
1811	Thomas dies.
	Hiokatoo dies.
1812	Jesse dies.
1817	John dies.
	Mary becomes a U.S. citizen.

1823	Mary tells her story to James Seaver.
1824	The first edition of *A Narrative of the Life of Mrs. Mary Jemison* is published.
1833	Mary Jemison dies. She was approximately eighty years old.

A NARRATIVE

OF THE LIFE OF

MRS. MARY JEMISON

WHO WAS TAKEN BY INDIANS IN THE YEAR 1758
WHEN SHE WAS ABOUT FIFTEEN YEARS OF AGE
WHO HAS CONTINUED TO RESIDE AMONGST
THEM TO THE PRESENT TIME
TAKEN FROM HER OWN WORDS
ON NOVEMBER 29, 1823

James E. Seaver

Introduction

BY JAMES E. SEAVER

The Peace Treaty of 1783, which ended the Revolutionary War and Indian hostilities, freed the prisoners who had spent many years in Indian captivity after surviving the threat of the tomahawk and the *running of the gauntlet*. This helped to restore harmony between the whites and the Indians on the frontier.

Stories of Indian cruelties were common in the new settlements before the treaty. Few Americans have reached middle age who cannot remember shrinking from fear as children while they listened to their parents or visitors relate stories of Indian conquests and murders. These tales would make the children's hair nearly stand erect.

At the close of the Revolutionary War, what is now western New York State was uninhabited by white people. Indeed, few had passed beyond Fort Stanwix near the state's eastern border except when engaged in war against the Indians before the revolution started, and some years passed after the war ended before land on the Genesee

River was visited by anyone except an occasional land speculator or by men and women who looked for the end of the earth to escape the law. At length, the rich soil encouraged emigration, and here and there a family settled, starting improvements in the country which had only recently been the property of the Indians.

Those who settled near the Genesee River soon became acquainted with "the White Woman," as Mrs. Jemison is called, whose history they eagerly sought. Frankness characterized her conduct, and without reserve, she would often relate some of the most important periods of her life. Although her closest friend was an old Indian warrior and her children and friends all Indians, it was found that she possessed an uncommon share of hospitality toward all people and that her friendship was well worth courting and preserving. Her house was the stranger's home, and she made welcome the weary wanderer. In all her actions there was much natural goodness of heart, and she became celebrated as the friend of the distressed. Many remember Mrs. Jemison's kindness toward them when they were prisoners during the war, and they credit their lives being saved to her intervention.

Several gentlemen, upon hearing her story, became most eager to publish her narrative. They wanted to preserve stories of Indian atrocities and to save some historical facts that otherwise might be lost.

In the autumn of 1823, when Mrs. Jemison had lived with the Indians nearly seventy years, one of these gentlemen, Daniel W. Banister, decided to add to his knowledge of Mrs. Jemison's life while she was still capable of recollecting and reciting the scenes through which she had passed. I was employed to collect the materials and prepare the work for the press.

I went to the house of Mrs. Jennet Whaley in Castile, New York, with the publisher, where Mary Jemison told us the story of her eventful life. She came a distance of four miles on foot in the company of Mr. Thomas Clute, a neighbor she trusts and depends upon for advice, and they stayed almost three days, during which time I was busily occupied in taking her narrative as she recited it. During this time, I could not help but compare her present situation with what her life probably would have been had she been permitted to remain with her family and friends.

Her appearance was quite agreeable to me. She is very short, and she stands tolerably erect with her head bent forward, apparently a result of carrying heavy burdens in a strap placed across her forehead. Formerly, her hair was a light brown. It is now quite gray, of middling length, and tied into a bunch behind her head. Her complexion is very white for a woman of her age, and although the wrinkles of eighty years are deeply indented in her cheeks, the crimson of youth is still visible. Her eyes are light blue, a little faded by age, but brilliant and sparkling. When she looks up and is engaged in conversation, her face is very expressive. Several times during her narration, tears trickled down her grief-worn cheek and at the same time, a rising sigh would stop her speech.

She speaks English plainly with a little of the Irish emphasis, and she will talk about any subject with which she is acquainted. Her recollection and memory exceeded my expectation. It cannot be reasonably supposed that a person of her age has kept the events of the past seventy

This portrait of Mary Jemison by Carlos Stebbins matches the description James Seaver gave, including her slightly stooped appearance, her delicate features, and her manner of dress: a shirt, short gown, moccasins, stockings, and Indian blanket. Courtesy of Letchworth State Park, Castile, New York.

years in so complete an order as to be able to assign to each its proper time and place. However, she gave her story with as few obvious mistakes as might be found in a person of fifty.

She is always busy. She pounds her *samp,* cooks for herself, gathers and chops wood, feeds her cattle and poultry, and performs other chores. Last season she planted, tended, and gathered corn.

Her dress was made and worn after the Indian fashion, and it consisted of a shirt, short gown, petticoat, stockings, moccasins, a blanket, and a bonnet. Her clothing was convenient and comfortable to wear, and she was contented with her garments. She wore them by choice, not as a matter of necessity, for her property is sufficient to enable her to dress in the best fashion and to allow her every comfort of life.

Her house is twenty by twenty-eight feet. It is built of square timber, and it has a shingled roof and a covered porch. In the center of the house are two fireplaces. She has a good barn, and she owns many cows and horses of the finest varieties. Besides the buildings mentioned, she owns a number of houses that are occupied by tenants who work her land upon *shares.*

Mrs. Jemison appeared sensitive about her ignorance of the ways of white people except with those with whom she was intimately acquainted. In fact, at first she appeared to be ill at ease with me as well as afraid of saying something that would be injurious to herself or her family. If Mr. Clute, whose advice she trusted completely, had not been present, I should probably have been unable to obtain her history.

However, after we had talked for a while, Mrs. Jemison became free and comfortable in her conversation. She spoke with a degree of mildness, candor, and simplicity that removes all doubt as to the truthfulness of the speaker. She seemed to take pride in extolling the Indians' virtues, and I believe family pride inclined her to withhold any information that would blot the character of her descendants. Pride may also have induced her to keep back many things that would have been interesting.

Her neighbors speak of her as possessing one of the happiest tempers and dispositions. To their knowledge, she has never committed a dishonorable act.

Mrs. Jemison's habits are those of Indians. She sleeps on skins, sits upon the floor or a bench, and holds her food on her lap or in her hands.

Her ideas of religion correspond in every respect with those of the Senecas. She applauds virtue and despises vice. She believes in a future life in which the good will be happy and the bad will be miserable, and she believes that a future life of happiness depends upon willingly doing good deeds. She is no longer familiar with the Christian religion.

Mrs. Jemison's descendants command respect. Her daughters are active, enterprising women, and her grandsons are considered able, decent men in their tribes.

Having in this brief manner introduced Mrs. Jemison, I now proceed to the narration of a life that has been viewed with interest for a number of years.

❦

ONE

A Forerunner
of
Catastrophe

My name is Mary Jemison. Although I may have frequently heard the history of my ancestry, my memory is too imperfect to enable me to trace it further back than to my father, Thomas Jemison, and my mother, Jane Erwin Jemison. However, I often heard them say that their families possessed wealth and honorable stations under the government of the country in which they lived. I am not able to state positively whether Ireland or Scotland was the land of my parents' birth and education, but it is my impression that they were born in Ireland.

My parents left their native land to escape civil wars and religious rules that prevented them from worshipping as they wanted. They and two sons and one daughter, John, Thomas, and Betsey, set sail for this country in 1742 or 1743 on the *Mary William*. I was born during the voyage.

Shortly after we arrived in Philadelphia, my father, being fond of rural life, moved his family to the then frontier settlements of Pennsylvania. He claimed a tract of excellent land next to Marsh Creek, where he cleared a large area, and for seven or eight years, he enjoyed the fruits of his hard work. During this time, my mother had two sons, between whose ages there were about three years. The oldest was named Matthew and the youngest was called Robert.

Our farm was a little paradise, and the happy days I spent there will ever stand fresh in my remembrance, even though I have passed through many severe trials since then. Frequently I dream of those days, but alas, they are gone. The recollection of my pleasant home and my family and the manner in which I was deprived of them all at once still affects me, and at times, I am almost overwhelmed with grief.

My parents were examples worthy of imitation. They were strict observers of religious duties, and it was the daily practice of my father to lead his family in worship morning and evening. Their affection for each other was mutual, and it was the happy kind that sweetens the cup of life and promotes not only their own comfort, but the comfort of all who knew them. I still remember their mildness and perfect agreement in the upbringing of their children, their mutual attention to our education, manners, wants, and religious instruction.

My education received as much attention from my parents as their situation would permit. I attended school some, where I learned to read in a book that was about half as large as a Bible. I also read a little of the Bible and learned the *catechism*, which I frequently repeated to my parents. Every night before I went to bed, I was obliged to stand before my mother and repeat some words that I suppose were a prayer.

I have long forgotten my reading, catechism, and prayers, although for a number of the first years that I lived with the Indians, I repeated my prayers as often as I had an opportunity to do so. After the Revolutionary War, I still remembered the names of some of the letters when I saw them, but I have not read a word since I was taken prisoner. A few years ago a missionary kindly gave me a Bible, which I am very fond of hearing my neighbors read to me. I should be pleased to learn to read it myself, but my sight has been dim for a number of years, and I can not distinguish one letter from another.

In the spring of 1752, the stories of Indian raids upon settlers' homes were common. These stories alarmed my parents, and they worried about our safety. Over the next years, the storm gathered faster. Many murders were committed, and many captives of the Indians met death in its most frightful form.

In 1754, the colonial government raised an army to protect the settlers on the frontier and drive the Indians and their ally, the French, away from the settlements. The army was placed under the command of Colonel George Washington. However, the French and Indians were victorious on the frontier in the beginning of the war, and after their victory over Colonel Washington at Great Meadows, they grew more and more terrible. The death of the whites and plundering and burning of their property become more common. But we had not heard the death yell or seen the smoke of a dwelling that had been lit by an Indian's hand.

New Year's Day, 1757, still found us unmolested, and

These Indians are shown waiting for the best moment to strike. Pioneers who lived far from forts or neighbors faced the greatest danger of attack. The farm in the background is typical of those in the Middle Colonies, which included Pennsylvania, Mary's home. Courtesy of Dover Pictorial Archive Series.

although we knew that the enemy was at no great distance from us, my father decided that he would continue to occupy his land another season. He expected, probably from the great efforts the colonial government was then making, that as soon as the troops could begin their operations in the spring, the enemy would be conquered and forced to agree to a peace treaty.

The winter of 1757–8 was as mild as a typical fall season, and spring came early. This meant that we could plant our seeds much earlier than expected, and with the longer growing season, we would probably have a bountiful harvest. My father and older brothers prepared the land for planting as usual. Father's cattle and sheep were numerous, and according to the best idea of wealth that I can now form, he was wealthy.

On a pleasant day in the spring of 1758, when my father was sowing *flaxseed* and my brothers were driving the teams, I was sent to a neighbor's house, a distance of perhaps a mile, to borrow a horse and return with it the next morning. I walked along rapidly, and as I neared our neighbors' house, I imagined that I saw what appeared to be a big white sheet rushing toward me. Suddenly I was caught up in a squall, a sudden violent gust of wind, and I was so frightened, I fainted.

My neighbors found me on the ground, almost lifeless, so they said. They took me in and made use of every remedy in their power for my recovery, but without effect until daybreak, when my senses returned. I soon found myself in good health, and I went home with the horse very early in the morning.

The appearance of that squall, I have ever believed, was a warning about the catastrophe that so soon afterwards happened to my family. My being caught up in the gust, I have no doubt, was an omen that I would not die when I was captured.

❦

TWO

A Sight
Most Appalling

When I got home, I found that a man who lived in our neighborhood and his sister-in-law and her three children had come to live with us for a short time, but for what reason, I cannot say. The woman's husband was in the colonial army, and she and her children were temporarily being housed on our neighbor's farm. Their names I have forgotten. Shortly after I arrived, the man took the horse I had borrowed from our neighbor to go to his house after a bag of grain. He took his gun in his hand for the purpose of killing game, if he should happen to see any.

My family, as usual, was busily employed. Father was working on an ax handle at the side of the house, and my two older brothers were at work near the barn. Mother was making preparations for breakfast, and the little ones and the woman and her three children were in the house. I immediately went inside.

Breakfast was not yet ready when we heard gunshots nearby. Mother and the woman almost fainted at the sound, and everyone trembled with fear. On opening the door, we saw the man who had gone to get grain and his horse lying dead near the house. They had just been shot by Indians. I was told afterwards by Mr. Fields, whom I saw many years after this event, that the Indians had discovered the man at his own house with his gun, and when he ran, they pursued him to Father's where he was shot.

While we stared in shock and disbelief, the Indians bound my father's arms, and then rushed into the house and without the least resistance made prisoners of my mother, Robert, Matthew, Betsey, the woman and her three children, and me. Then they began to plunder our home, taking what they considered most valuable, as much bread, meal, and meat as they could carry.

My two brothers, Thomas and John, who were at work near the barn, escaped. I was later told that they eventually went to Virginia, where my grandfather lived.

The party that took us consisted of six Indians and four Frenchmen who then set out with their prisoners in great haste, fearing detection. Shortly after, we entered a woods. On our march that day, an Indian went behind us with a whip which he used to lash the children to make them keep up. We traveled until dark without a mouthful of food or a drop of fresh water, although we had not eaten since the night before. Whenever the little children cried for water, the Indians made them drink urine or go thirsty.

That night we camped in the woods without a fire or shelter. We were watched with the greatest vigilance. Exhausted and very hungry, we were forced to lie upon the ground without food and without a drop of water to satisfy the cravings or our appetites. Fatigue alone brought us a little sleep.

At dawn, we again started to march in the same order that we had proceeded on the day before. About sunrise we halted, and the Indians gave us a full breakfast from *provision* that they had brought from my father's house. Each of us, being very hungry, partook of this meal except Father, who was overcome with the situation. He was exhausted by anxiety, grief, and despair, and he could not be prevailed upon to ease his pain a little with food.

When we finished eating, we once again resumed our march, and before noon we passed a small fort that Father said was called Fort Canagojigge. That was the only time I heard him speak from the time we were taken until we were finally separated the following night.

Towards evening, we arrived at the edge of a dark, dismal, swampy area, which was covered with small hemlocks, or some other evergreen, and a variety of bushes. We were led into the darkness, and after going a short distance, we stopped to rest for the night. Here we were given some bread and meat for supper, but the dreariness of our situation together with the uncertainty about our future almost deprived us of our appetites.

Mother, from the time we were taken, had shown great fortitude, and she encouraged us to face our troubles

In 1758 Mary Jemison was taken captive on her family farm in what is now southern Pennsylvania. Her captors took her to Fort Duquesne, where she was given to two Seneca squaws who then took her to their village, Mingo Town, located on the Ohio River. Map by Karen Zeinert.

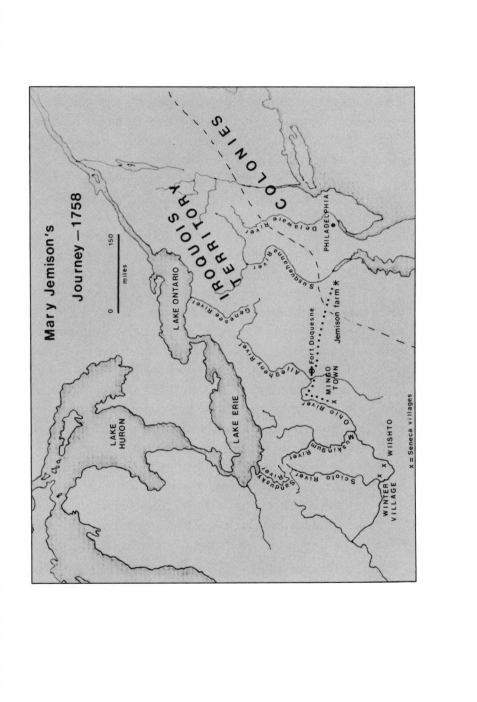

Mary Jemison's
Journey — 1758

IROQUOIS TERRITORY

COLONIES

LAKE HURON

LAKE ERIE

LAKE ONTARIO

Genesee River

Allegheny River

Susquehanna River

Delaware River

PHILADELPHIA

Fort Duquesne

Jemison farm ✱

MINGO TOWN

Ohio River

Muskingum River

Scioto River

Sandusky River

WINTER VILLAGE

WIISHTO

x = Seneca villages

0   150
miles

without complaining. Her conversation seemed to make the distance and time shorter and the trail smoother. That evening, as she had done before, she insisted that we eat. We obeyed her, but it was done with heavy hearts. Father had lost all his ambition in the beginning, and he continued to be absorbed in melancholy.

As soon as I had finished my supper, an Indian took off my shoes and stockings. He then put a pair of moccasins on my feet.

My mother watched carefully, and believing that it was a sign that my life would be spared, she addressed me, as near as I can remember, in the following words:

"My dear little Mary, I fear that the time has arrived when we must be parted forever. Your life, my child, I think will be spared, but we will probably be murdered here in this lonesome place. How can I part with you my darling? What will become of my sweet little Mary? How can I bear to think of you being held in captivity without any hope of being rescued? O that death had snatched you from my arms in your infancy! The pain of parting then would have been pleasing to what it is now, and I should have seen the end of your troubles. My heart bleeds at the thought of what awaits you.

"If you are taken from us, my child, always remember your own name and the name of your father and mother. Do not forget your English tongue. If you have an opportunity to get away from the Indians, don't try to escape, for if you do, they will find and destroy you. Don't forget the prayers that I have taught you. Say them often. Be a good child, and God will bless you, my darling, and make you comfortable and happy."

While she was talking, the Indians stripped the

shoes and stockings from the little boy who belonged to the woman who was taken with us, and they put moccasins on his feet, too. When an Indian took the little boy and me by the hand and began to lead us away from the company, I started to cry.

Mother saw my tears and exclaimed, "Don't cry, Mary! Don't cry, my child. God will bless you! Farewell! Farewell!"

The Indian led us some distance into the bushes, and he lay down with us to spend the night. The recollection of parting with my mother kept me awake, and the tears constantly flowed from my eyes. A number of times in the night, the little boy begged me to run away with him, but I remembered the advice Mother had given me. I knew the dangers to which we would be exposed while traveling without a path or guide through a wilderness unknown to us, and I told him that I would not go.

Early the next morning, the Indians and the Frenchmen we had left the night before came to us without our families. It is impossible for anyone to form a correct idea of what my feelings were at the sight of those savages who I supposed had murdered my parents, brothers, sister, and friends and left them in the swamp to be devoured by wild beasts!

But what could I do? I had no power or means of escaping, no home to go to even if I could escape, and I didn't have any family to whom I could fly to for protection. I felt a kind of horror, anxiety, and dread that seemed unbearable. But I durst not cry; I durst not complain. And to inquire about the fate of my family, even if I could have mustered the courage, was beyond my ability. I could not speak their languages, and they did not understand mine. My only relief was in silent, stifled sobs.

My awful suspicion as to the fate of my parents proved too true; soon after I left them, they were killed and scalped, together with Robert, Matthew, Betsey and the woman and her two children. All were mangled in the most shocking manner, so I learned many years later.

After giving the little boy and me some bread and meat for breakfast, our captors led us on as fast as we could travel. One of them went behind with a long staff, picking up all the grasses and weeds that we had tramped upon. By taking that precaution, they avoided detection. It is the custom of Indians when scouting or on private expeditions to step carefully, avoiding any spot where an impression of their feet can be left. Thus they shun wet or muddy ground. They seldom take hold of a bush or limb, and they never break one. By observing those precautions and setting up any weeds and grasses they might flatten, they leave no trail, thus eluding their pursuers.

After a hard day's march we camped in a thicket where the Indians made a shelter of boughs. They built a good fire to warm our numbed limbs and dry our clothing, which was wet from showers that occurred throughout the day. Here we were fed as before.

When the Indians had finished their supper, they took from their baggage a number of scalps, and they began to dress them for the market or to keep them from spoiling. First they put the wet, bloody scalps over small hoops, which they made for that purpose, and they stretched the scalps to their full extent. They then held the scalps near the fire until they were partly dried, at which time they used their knives to scrape away flesh.

They continued to work in that way, alternately drying and scraping, until the scalps were clean. That being done, they combed the hair in the neatest manner, and then they painted it and the edges of the scalps, yet on the hoops, red.

I knew those scalps had been taken from my family by the color of the hair. My mother's hair was red, and I could easily distinguish my father's and the children's from each other. That sight was most appalling, yet I had no choice but to endure it without complaining.

In the course of the night, my captors made me to understand that they would not have killed the others if the whites had not pursued them. I later found out that on hearing of our captivity, the whole neighborhood turned out in pursuit of the enemy in order to rescue us. Our neighbors had followed us as far as the swamp, where they found the bodies, but they could no longer trace us.

The next morning we went on, an Indian going behind us, setting up weeds as on the day before. At night we camped on the ground without a shelter or fire.

In the morning, we again set out early. We traveled as on the two former days, through the weather was extremely uncomfortable due to a spring storm that produced rain or snow all day long. That evening, snow fell fast, and the Indians built a shelter of boughs and lit a fire. We rested tolerably well there throughout the night. Halted by the storm, we spent two more nights in this shelter.

While we were there, six Indians who had been to the frontier settlements came to us. They brought with them a prisoner, a young white man whose name I have

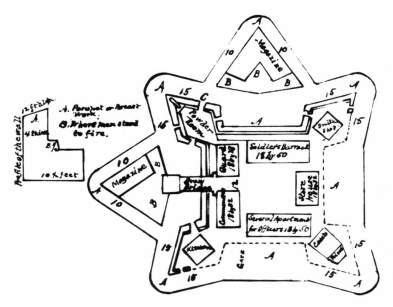

Fort Duquesne, a site for meetings, trading, and protection, was well fortified. It was surrounded by a picket fence made from logs standing twelve feet high. The top of each log was sharpened to a fine point. A ditch, represented by the letter A *in the diagram, was dug outside and close to the fence for additional protection. (Only a few mounds of earth were left, and these are labeled with the letter* B*). For invaders to scale the fence they had to scramble out of the ditch while being shot at. The numbers are an estimate of size, given in feet. Mary would have been taken into the fort through the gate, located at the bottom of the diagram, on the side of the fort facing the Ohio River. She was probably held in the small prison at the bottom right. Diagram by Robert Stobo in* Frontier Forts of Pennsylvania *(1896). Courtesy of the Historical Society of Western Pennsylvania.*

forgotten, who was very tired and dejected. I was extremely glad to see him. However, I knew from his appearance that his situation was as deplorable as mine and that he could give me no assistance.

That afternoon, the Indians killed a deer, which they roasted whole after dressing it out. We were allowed a share of their venison and some bread, so that we made a good meal also.

When the storm ceased, the whole company, twelve Indians, four Frenchmen, the young man, the little boy, and I, resumed our march. Knowing that the storm has destroyed any previous trail we might have left, the Indians felt secure, and our party moved at a moderate pace without an Indian behind us to deceive any pursuers.

In the afternoon, we came in sight of Fort Pitt, as it is now called. That fort was occupied then by the French and Indians, and they called it Fort Duquesne. It stood at the junction of the Monongahela and Allegheny rivers, where the Ohio River begins. Here we halted while the Indians performed some customs upon their prisoners, which they deemed necessary. The Indians combed our hair and then painted our hair and faces red in the finest Indian style. We were then conducted into the fort. After we received a little bread, we were locked in a room where we spent the night alone.

❦

THREE

She Is Our Sister

The night was spent in gloomy forebodings. What our future held was out of our power to determine, but this didn't keep us from imagining what might happen. At times we could almost see our masters approaching, intent on butchering and scalping us or roasting us upon a pile of wood. Then we would imagine ourselves at liberty, but alone and defenseless in the forest, surrounded by wild beasts that were ready to devour us. Our anxiety made it impossible for us to sleep, and it was with a dreadful hope and painful impatience that we waited for the morning when we would learn our fate.

The morning at length arrived, and our masters came early to let us out of the house. They gave the young man and boy to the French, who immediately took them away. Their fate I never learned, as I have not seen nor heard of them since.

I was now alone, deprived of my former companions and everything that was near and dear to me except life. But it was not long before I was in some measure relieved by the appearance of two pleasant-looking squaws of the Seneca tribe, who examined me attentively for a short time and then went out. After a few minutes, they returned with my masters, who gave me to them to dispose of as they pleased.

The Indians by whom I was taken were Shawnees, if I remember right, who lived a long distance down the Ohio River. They and the two squaws were now ready to leave the fort. The Indians, in a large canoe, and the two squaws and I, in a small one, started down the river. One of the Shawnees took the scalps of my family, strung them on a pole that he placed upon his shoulder, and stood in the back of the canoe directly before us as we sailed down the river to the town where the two squaws lived.

On our way, we passed a Shawnee town. Here I saw a number of heads, arms, legs, and other fragments of bodies of some white people who had just been roasted. The fire was yet burning, and the scene was so shocking that, even to this day, my blood almost curdles in my veins when I think of it!

That night we arrived at a small Seneca village, Mingo Town, at the mouth of a small river that is called She-nan-jee by the Indians, where the two squaws lived. We landed here, and the Shawnees went on, the last I ever saw of them.

Having made fast to the shore, the squaws left me in the canoe while they went to their wigwam in the town. They returned with a suit of Indian clothing, all new and very clean and nice. My clothes, though whole and good when I was taken, were now torn into pieces, so that I was almost naked. They undressed me, threw

This village is typical of America's Eastern woodland Indians. While each had its own unique way of living, the woodland tribes had some similar customs. The Senecas of Mingo Town, for example, lived in wigwams, raised corn, squash, and pumpkins, wore clothing fashioned from deerskins, pounded corn meal with wooden tools as the woman in the foreground is doing, lived beside the water, and traveled by canoe just as the Indians in this village did. Courtesy of the Department of Library Services, American Museum of Natural History, New York. Neg. 312686; photo by H. S. Rice.

my rags into the river, washed me clean, and dressed me in Indian style Then they led me home and seated me in the center of their wigwam.

I had been in that situation but a few minutes before all the squaws in the town came to see me. They surrounded me and immediately began a most dismal howling, crying bitterly, and wringing their hands in agony and grief for a deceased relative. Their tears flowed freely, and they showed all the signs of real mourning.

At the beginning of this scene, one of them began to recite some words in a voice somewhat between speaking and singing, and the others varied the appearance of their faces, gestures, and tone of their voices to correspond with the sentiments expressed:

"Oh, our brother! Alas! He is dead—he has gone; he will never return! Friendless he died on the field of the slain, where his bones are yet lying unburied! Oh, who will not mourn his sad fate? No tears dropped around him. Oh, no! No tears of his sisters were there! He fell in his prime, when he was most needed to keep us from danger! Alas! He has gone and left us in sorrow! Oh, where is his spirit? His spirit went naked, and hungry it wanders, and thirsty and wounded it groans to return! He has no blanket to warm him, no food to nourish him, no candles to light his way, no weapons to defend himself.

"Well we remember his deeds. The deer he could take in the chase! The panther shrank back at the sight of his strength! His enemies fell at his feet! He was brave and courageous in war! His war whoop was shrill! His rifle well aimed laid his enemies low. His tomahawk drank of their blood, and his knife flayed their scalps while yet covered with gore. Yet like a fawn he was harmless. His friendship was ardent; his temper was gentle; his pity was great!

"But why do we mourn? He fell on the field of the slain with glory, and his spirit went up to the land of his fathers in war. With joy they received him, fed him, clothed him, and welcomed him there. Oh, friends, he is happy. Dry up your tears!

"His spirit has seen our distress, and it sent us a helper whom we greet with pleasure. Let us receive her with joy! She is handsome and pleasant. Oh, she is our sister, and gladly we welcome her here. In the place of our brother she stands in our tribe. We will guard her from trouble. May she be happy until her spirit shall leave us."

In the course of that ceremony, they became serene. Joy sparkled in their eyes, and they seemed to rejoice over me as if I were a long lost child. I was made welcome among them as a sister to the two squaws. They called me Deh-ge-wan-us, which means "two voices falling." This is the name by which I have ever since been called by the Indians.

I learned afterwards that the ceremony I passed through was that of adoption. It is a custom of the Indians, when one of their number is slain or taken prisoner in battle, to give the nearest relative a prisoner if the warriors have taken one or a scalp of the enemy if no one was captured. On the return of the Indians from conquest, which is always announced by shouting, demonstrations of joy, and the exhibition of some trophy of victory, the mourners come forward and make their claims.

If they receive a prisoner, it is their decision either to take revenge by killing the prisoner in the most cruel manner they can devise, or they may adopt him into the family to take the place of the warrior they have lost. Unless the mourners have just received the news of their loss and are full of grief and thirsty for revenge, or unless the prisoner is very old or sickly, they generally save him and treat him kindly. But if a family's pain is fresh and its loss so great that it deems it irreparable, no torture, no matter how cruel, seems sufficient to satisfy them. It is the action of grieving family members, and not the nation, that has caused others to call Indians "barbarians." The two squaws had lost a brother in a battle against the English, and as a result, they went to Fort Duquesne the day I arrived in order to receive a prisoner or an enemy's scalp to ease their loss.

During my adoption, I sat motionless, nearly terri- fied to death at the appearance and actions of the women. I expected to feel their vengeance at any moment and suffer death on the spot. I was, however, happily disap- pointed when at the close of the ceremony, the company left, and my sisters went about employing every means for my consolation and comfort. I was, from then on, treated as a real sister, the same as though I had been born of their mother.

Being now settled and provided with a home and family that included three brothers who lived elsewhere in the village, I tried to adjust to my new life. My situa- tion was easy, and I had no particular hardships to en- dure. I helped care for young children in the village, and I did light work about the wigwam. Occasionally I was sent out with the hunters when they went but a short distance to help them carry their game. Still, the memory of my parents, my brothers and sisters, my home, and my own captivity destroyed my happiness and made me lonesome and gloomy.

My sisters would not allow me to speak English while I was around them; but remembering the charge that my dear mother gave me at the time I left her, when- ever I was alone, I repeated my prayers, catechism, or something I had learned in order that I might not forget my own language. By practicing in that way, I retained some English. Later when I came to the *Genesee flats*, where I became acquainted with English people with whom I visit almost daily, I was able to improve my English a great deal.

My sisters were diligent in teaching me their language. To their great satisfaction, I learned quickly, and soon I could understand their language readily and speak it fluently.

I was very fortunate in falling into their hands, for they were kind, good-natured women, peaceable and mild in their dispositions, temperate and decent in their habits, and very tender and gentle towards me. I have great reason to respect them though they have been dead a great number of years.

The town where they lived was pleasant and prosperous. The land produced good corn; the woods furnished an abundance of game, and the waters abounded with fish. We spent the summer at that place, where we planted, hoed, and harvested a large crop of corn of excellent quality.

When the corn was harvested, the Indians took it on horses and in canoes down the Ohio, occasionally stopping to hunt a few days until we arrived at the mouth of the Scioto River. Here they established their winter quarters, where the hunting was good. I went with the children to assist them in bringing in their game. The forests along the river were well stocked with elk, deer, and other large animals, and the nearby marshes contained large numbers of beaver and muskrat. Indians depended upon elk and deer for their meat and beaver and

The Senecas raised at least twelve different varieties of corn. Some varieties were best eaten fresh, others were raised for corn meal or storage. The Senecas were extremely successful at growing corn, and some ears reached twenty *inches in length.*

Corn was prepared in many ways. It could be made into soup, corn bread, corn pudding, or gruel, which is similar to oatmeal. Beans were often added to soup, making succotash, a popular dish, and nuts, berries, and maple syrup were added to puddings to give them extra flavor. Courtesy of John A. Zeinert.

muskrat for furs that could be traded for ammunition and clothing.

In the spring, we all returned to Mingo Town to the houses and fields we had left the fall before. Again we planted our corn, squashes, and beans on the fields that we occupied the preceding summer.

About planting time, our Indians went to Fort Duquesne, now under English control and renamed Fort Pitt, to assure the British, who had defeated the French and their Indian allies in the area, that we wanted peace. The Indians took me with them. We landed on the opposite side of the river from the fort and camped there for the night. Early the next morning, the Indians took me over to the fort to see the white people who were there. It was then that my heart bounded to be liberated from the Indians and to be restored to my friends and my country.

The white people were surprised to see me with the Indians, enduring their hard life at so early an age with so delicate a constitution as I appeared to possess. They asked me my name and where and when I was taken, and they appeared very much interested on my behalf. When they continued their inquiries, my sisters became alarmed, believing that I was about to be taken from them. They hurried me into their canoe and fled with me without stopping until they arrived at the Shenanjee River.

I was informed later by one of my Indian brothers that shortly after my sisters and I left the fort, the white people came over to our camp to take me back. After failing to find me after making a diligent search, they returned to the fort with heavy hearts.

Although I had been with the Indians something over a year and had become used to their way of living and attached to my sisters, the sight of white people who could speak English had filled me with an unspeakable anxiety to go home with them. My sudden departure and escape from them seemed like a second captivity, and for a long time I brooded at the thought of my miserable situation with almost as much sorrow and dejection as I had when I first arrived. Time eventually wore away my unpleasant feelings, however, and I became as contented as before.

We tended our cornfields through the summer, and after we had harvested the crop, we again went down the river to the hunting grounds on the Scioto. Here we spent the winter, as we had done the winter before.

🌿

FOUR

I Loved Him

E arly in the spring, we sailed up the Ohio River to a place that the Indians called Wiishto. Here the Indians built a new town, and we planted corn in new fields [that would produce more heavily than those near Mingo Town, which had been depleted by repeated use].

During our first summer at Wiishto, a party of Delaware Indians came up the river, took up their residence, and lived in common with us. They brought five white prisoners with them, who, by their conversation, made my situation much more agreeable, as they could all speak English.

Not long after the Delawares came to live with us, my sisters told me that I must go and live with one of them, She-nin-jee. Not daring to cross them or disobey their commands, I went, but with a great degree of reluctance; Sheninjee and I were married according to Indian custom.

Sheninjee was a noble man, large in stature, elegant in his appearance, generous in his conduct, courageous in war, a believer in peace, and a great lover of justice. He merited and received the confidence and friendship of all the tribes with whom he was acquainted. Yet Sheninjee was an Indian. The idea of spending my days with him at first offended my feelings and greatly upset me. But his good nature, generosity, tenderness, and friendship towards me soon gained my affection. To me he was ever kind in sickness, and he always treated me with gentleness. In fact, he was an agreeable husband and a comfortable companion. And strange as it may seem, I loved him! We lived happily together until the time of our final separation, which happened two or three years after our marriage.

In our second summer at Wiishto, I had a child at the time that kernels of corn first appeared on the cob. When the time came to deliver my baby, Sheninjee was absent, and I was taken to a small shed on the bank of the river, which was made of boughs, until my husband returned. My two sisters attended me, and on the second day of my confinement my child, a girl, was born. She lived only two days, and it was a great grief to me to lose her.

After the birth of my child, I was very sick, but I was not allowed to go into the house for two weeks. Then to my great joy, Sheninjee returned, and I was taken home and as comfortably provided for as our situation would permit. My illness continued to increase for a number of days. I became so weak, my recovery was despaired of by my friends, and I concluded that my troubles would soon be finished. At length, however, my condition took a favorable turn, and by the time the corn was ripe, I was able to get about. I continued to regain my health, and in the fall, I was able to go to our winter quarters on the Scioto.

From that time on, nothing remarkable occurred to me until the fourth winter of my captivity, when I had a son. I had a quick recovery, and my child was healthy. To commemorate the name of my much lamented father, I called my son Thomas Jemison.

In the spring when Thomas was three or four *moons* old, we returned to Wiishto again. I had then been with the Indians four summers and four winters, and I had become so accustomed to their way of living that my eagerness to get away, to be set free, had almost subsided. With them was my home. My family was there, and I had many friends to whom I was warmly attached because of the favors, affection, and friendship with which they had uniformly treated me from the time of my adoption.

Our labor was not severe, and the work of one year was exactly the same, in almost every respect, to that of the others without that endless variety observed in the common labor of the white people. Indian women do have to bring in all the fuel and cook all the food, but their tasks are not any harder than that of white women, and their cares certainly are not half as numerous nor as great.

When we planted, tended, and harvested our corn, we generally had all our children with us. We had no master to oversee or drive us, so we could work as leisurely as we pleased. We had no plows, but performed the whole process of planting and hoeing with a small tool that resembled a hoe with a very short handle.

Our cooking chores consisted of pounding our corn

The Senecas divided a year into nine segments based on the lunar calendar. They began their new year after the last full moon of winter, about the end of January, with the Maple Moon. This was followed by the Frog Moon, the Planting Moon, the Strawberry Moon, the Moon of Green Corn, the Corn Harvest Moon, the Moon of Falling Leaves, the Moon of Long Nights, and the Starving Moon, four of which are represented here by berries, seeds, leaves, and freshly picked corn still in its husks. Courtesy of John A. Zeinert.

into samp or *hominy,* boiling the hominy, now and then making a *cake* and baking it in hot ashes, and boiling or roasting our venison. Since our cooking and eating utensils consisted of a hominy *block and pestle,* a small kettle, a knife or two, and a few vessels of bark or wood, it required but little time to keep them in order for use.

Spinning, weaving, sewing, knitting, and the like are white women's arts, and they have seldom been practiced in the Indian tribes. After the Revolutionary War, I learned to sew so that I could make my own clothing after a poor fashion, but I am not acquainted with the other domestic arts such as spinning and weaving.

During hunting season, it was our business, in addition to our cooking, to bring home the game that was taken by the hunters, dress it, and carefully preserve the edible meat, and prepare or dress the skins for clothing. This was fastened together with strings of deerskin and tied on with the same.

In that manner we lived, without any of those jealousies, quarrels, and revengeful battles between families and individuals, which have been common in the Indian tribes since the introduction of ardent spirits amongst them.

The use of liquor amongst the Indians and the attempts which have been made to civilize and Christianize them by the white people have constantly made them worse and worse. These attempts have increased the Indians' vices and robbed them of many of their virtues; both efforts will ultimately produce their extermination. I have seen, in a number of instances, the effects of education upon some of our Indians who were taken from their families when they were young and placed in schools before they had had an opportunity to contract many Indian habits, remaining there until they reached manhood. I have never seen one of these who wasn't an Indian in every respect after he returned. Indians must and will be Indians, in spite of all the means that can be used for their cultivation in the sciences and arts.

Only one thing marred my happiness while I lived with the Indians on the Ohio and that was the recollection that I had once had tender parents and a home that I loved. Aside from that consideration, or if I had been taken in infancy, I should have been contented in my situation. Notwithstanding all that has been said against the Indians in consequence of their cruelties to their enemies—cruelties that I have witnessed—it is a fact that they are naturally kind, tender, and peaceable toward their friends and strictly honest. The cruelties have been practiced only upon their enemies, according to the Indians' idea of justice.

🌱

FIVE

Dreadful Thoughts Haunted My Imagination

[Mary's Seneca family had relatives in Genishau, a large settlement situated on the Genesee River where Geneseo, New York, is now located. Her two sisters and mother had moved there two years earlier, and Mary, her husband and son, and two of Mary's brothers wanted to go to Fort Pitt to sell some pelts and buy some necessities and then travel to Genishau to visit relatives for the winter. Mary did not state how they planned to reach this village. She does mention, however, that they started up the river to the fort, and this river is most likely the Ohio, which would have been the easiest route. Whatever their plans might have been, they were changed before they reached the fort.]

Our party embarked in a canoe that was large enough to hold us and our effects, and we proceeded on our voyage up the river.

Nothing remarkable occurred to us on our way until we arrived at the mouth of a creek where two or three

English fur traders had a trading post. We had paddled upstream past the post but a short distance when we saw three white men, who appeared to have been recently murdered by Indians, floating down the river. We supposed them to be the bodies of the traders whose post we had just passed. Sheninjee was afraid of being apprehended as one of the murderers if we should go on, so we abandoned our plans to go to Fort Pitt, and we put about immediately and headed to the trading post.

At the store, we found the party of Shawnee Indians who had murdered the traders a few hours before. These Indians had come to plunder the store. When we arrived, they were torturing a young white man they had captured. At first, they made him stand up while they slowly pared his ears and split them into strings. Then they made a number of cuts on his face, bound him, rolled him in dirt and rubbed dirt into his wounds. Some of them whipped him with small rods at the same time. The poor fellow cried for mercy and yelled most piteously.

The sight of his distress was too much for me to endure. I repeatedly begged the Shawnees to desist, and at length they set him free. The prisoner was shockingly disfigured, bled profusely, and appeared to be in great pain, but as soon as he was liberated, he made off in great haste.

After a short stay at that place, we decided to take a pleasure trip before starting back to Wiishto. We went up the Candusky Creek about forty miles to a Shawnee town, and we stayed there but a few days before heading to Yiskahwana, which means "open mouth" in English. While we were there, my third brother arrived from Genishau, and insisted so strenuously upon our going to Genishau that once again my two other brothers decided to go and take me with them.

By this time, the summer was gone, and the time for harvesting corn had arrived. My brothers, for fear of the rainy season setting in early, thought it best to set out immediately so that we might have good traveling. Sheninjee wanted to go down the river and sell our pelts, then spend the winter in hunting with his friends. He consented to have me go on with my brothers. After promising to come to Genishau in the spring, he set out for Wiishto. My three brothers and I, with my little son on my back, began our long trip to Genishau.

Shortly after, we came to an Indian town on the Upper Sandusky River that had been deserted by its inhabitants. The Indians had recently murdered some English traders who resided among them, and fearing punishment if caught, had fled. This town was owned and had been occupied by Delawares, who when they left it, buried their provision in the ground in order to preserve it from their enemies or to have it for themselves if they should chance to return.

My brothers understood the Delawares' customs, and suspecting that their corn must have been hidden, made diligent search. At length they found a large quantity of it, together with beans, sugar, and honey, so carefully buried that it was completely dry and as good as when they left it. As our stock was scanty, we considered ourselves extremely fortunate in finding such a supply. Having caught two or three horses that we found there to carry our store of food, we traveled on.

But our long trip was not easy. Only those who have traveled on foot the distance of five or six hundred miles through an almost pathless wilderness can form an idea of the fatigue and sufferings that I endured on that journey. The fall rains came, and my clothing was thin and did little to protect me from the continually drenching rains. At night with nothing but my wet blanket to cover me, I had to sleep on the naked ground, without a shelter, unless nature provided some cover. In addition, I had to carry my child, then about nine months old, on my back or in my arms every step of the journey, and I had to provide for his comfort and prevent his suffering as best I could. I was so tired sometimes, I felt that it was impossible for me to continue. But my brothers were attentive, and eventually we reached Genishau in good health, and without having experienced a day's sickness since we left.

We were kindly received by my Indian mother and the other members of my family. My sisters, whom I had not seen in two years, received me with every expression of love and friendship, and I have never had the least reason to doubt that they really felt what they expressed. The warmth of their feelings, their kindness, and the continued favors that I received at their hands strengthened my affection for them so much, I truly believe that I loved them as I should have loved my own sister had she lived.

When we arrived at Genishau, the warriors there were making preparations to help the French retake Fort Niagara from the British, who had taken it from the French the month before in a war [French and Indian War, 1756–63] that had now lasted nearly six years. The warriors marched off the day after we arrived, determined on death or victory.

The British, confident that their hold on Fort Niag-

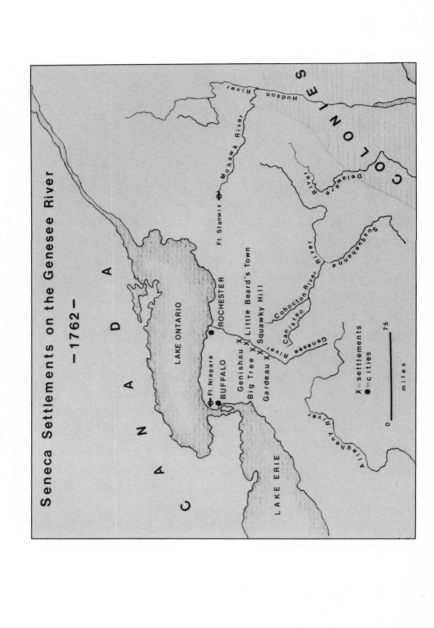

Seneca Settlements on the Genesee River

—1762—

CANADA

LAKE ONTARIO

LAKE ERIE

COLONIES

Hudson River

Mohawk River

Delaware River

Ft. Stanwix

ROCHESTER

BUFFALO

Ft. Niagara

Genishau X
Big Tree X
Gardeau X

X Little Beard's Town
X Squawky Hill

Cohocton River

Canisteo River

Genesee River

Susquehanna River

Allegheny River

X = settlements
● = cities

0   75
miles

ara was secure, now decided to take Fort Schlosser, lying a few miles up the river from Niagara. A large detachment of soldiers was sent out from Niagara to secure it. However, on their way, they were surrounded by French soldiers and Indian warriors who lay in ambush, and they were driven off the bank of a river into a place called the Devil's Hole together with their horses, carriages, and artillery. Not a single man escaped.

Our Indians returned in triumph, bringing with them two white prisoners and a number of oxen. These were the first oxen ever brought to the Genesee flats.

The next day was set aside as a day of feasting and celebrating, a preparation for the torture and execution of the two prisoners, upon whom the Indians planned to take out their revenge. One of my sisters was eager to attend the execution, and she wanted to take me with her to witness the customs of the warriors, as it was one of their most important ceremonies, one that was not often attended with so much pomp and parade as it was expected this would be. I had never attended an execution, and I felt a kind or horrid dread. My heart revolted at the very thought of watching someone being tortured to death.

On the morning of the execution, my sister told our mother that she would take me to see the prisoners die. Our mother objected strongly and with feeling:

Many Seneca Indians lived on the Genesee River in 1762 in what is now New York State. In order for Mary to reach Genishau, she and her brothers traveled many miles on foot. After leaving the Sandusky River (see previous map in Chapter 2), they headed east through a wilderness area, until they reached the Genesee River. Map by Karen Zeinert.

The Genesee River area is a picturesque site with roaring water-falls and forests of towering, fragrant pines. Courtesy of Letch-worth State Park, Castile, New York.

"How, my daughter," she said, addressing my sister, "can you even think of seeing the unspeakable torments that those poor prisoners must suffer? And how can you think of taking your poor sister Dehgewanus to see such a sight, she who has so lately been a prisoner herself and who has lost her family at the hands of bloody warriors! How can you think of making her bleed at the wounds that are now only partly healed? The memory of her ordeal would deprive us of Dehgewanus, for she would surely die after witnessing such a scene. We have nothing to do with war. Our husbands and brothers are proud to defend us, and their hearts beat with ardor to meet our foes. Stay then, my daughter. Let our warriors alone perform their customs of war on their victims!"

This speech had the desired effect. We remained at home and attended to our duties rather than watching the prisoners' executions.

I spent the winter comfortably and as agreeably as I could have expected to in the absence of my kind husband. But when spring came, Sheninjee did not appear, and when summer came, he still had not found me. I was confident that his love for me was so great that if he was alive, he would follow me, and I should see him again. Now dreadful thoughts haunted my imagination, and I worried about his well-being.

Toward the end of the summer, I received the message I had feared. Shortly after Sheninjee had left me at Yiskahwana, he was taken sick, and he died later at Wiishto. This was a heavy and unexpected blow. I was now left a widow with a son, with both of us entirely dependent on me for survival. My mother, sisters, and brothers did all they could to help me. Eventually my grief wore off, and I again became contented.

A year or two after this, the King of England offered a reward to anyone who would bring prisoners taken in the French and Indian War to any military post. John Van Sice, a Dutchman who had frequently been at our place and was well acquainted with every prisoner at Genishau, decided to take me to Niagara to collect this bounty. I was told of his intention, but since I was determined not to be taken in at that time, especially with his help, I watched his movements in order to avoid falling into his hands.

As it happened, he saw me alone at work in the cornfield shortly after, and thinking he could secure me easily, he ran toward me in great haste. I saw him coming and knowing what he planned, I ran from him with all the speed I had. He gave up the chase eventually, but I, fearing that he might be lying in wait for me, hid in an old cabin for three days and nights. When I went back, I walked slowly, looking for Van Sice, fearing he might apprehend me at any moment. But I got home without difficulty.

Soon after, the chiefs in council, having learned the cause of my running away, gave orders that I should not be taken to any military post against my will. They announced that since it was my choice to stay, I should live among them quietly and undisturbed.

Even so, only a few days later, the old king of our tribe told one of my brothers, Black Coals, that he planned to take me to Niagara himself. My brother said that I should not be taken to the fort and that I should

Elected representatives from Seneca villages met regularly in council houses such as this one, which now stands in Letchworth State Park on the Genesee River, to make decisions for their people. This procedure was followed by all six nations of the Iroquois League, which also elected representatives to the Great Council. The Iroquois established the first democracy in North America.

When Mary was first taken captive, most Indian shelters were made from bark. As settlers moved into the area and the Senecas lost their vast lands and their ability to move every few years, they built more permanent dwellings—log cabins. Courtesy of Letchworth State Park, Castile, New York.

be able to stay with the tribe as long as I wanted. A serious quarrel took place between them, and my brother told the old king that he would kill me with his own hands rather than have me taken by force to the fort. My brother then went to my sister's house, where I now lived, and informed her of all that had happened. He told her that he firmly believed that the old king would attempt to take me. Black Coals repeated his vow to kill me no matter what the consequences would be for him. He then returned to the old king to try to persuade him to leave me alone.

As soon as I came in, my sister told me what she had heard. Anxious for my safety, she told me to take my son and hide in some high weeds a short distance from the house. My brother had said that he would return in the evening and let my sister know the final conclusion of the matter, and she promised to inform me. When all was silent in the house, she said that I should creep softly to the door. If my brother planned to kill me, she would place a cake by the entry, and I was to take the cake and my child and go as fast as I could to a large spring on the south side of Samp's Creek, a place I had often seen, and wait there until I heard from her. If no cake could be found near the entry, I was to go in, for this meant that the old king had abandoned his plan.

I instantly followed her advice and went into the weeds, where I lay in a state of the greatest anxiety until nightfall. When it was quiet in the house, I crept to the door, and there I found—to my great distress!—a little cake. I then crept back to the weeds where I had hidden my son, and I put him on my back and made my course for the spring as fast as my legs would carry me.

I got to the spring early in the morning, almost overcome with fatigue, fearing that I might be pursued and taken at any moment. Thomas was nearly three years old and very large and heavy. Carrying him all the way had exhausted me. I sat down with my child at the spring, and he and I made a breakfast of the little cake and drank water from the spring.

That morning, the old king came to our house in search of me. When he could not find me, he gave up and went to Niagara with the prisoners he had already taken.

As soon as the danger had passed, my sister told my brother where he could find me. He immediately set out for the spring, and he reached me about noon. The first sight of him made me tremble with the fear of death, but when he came close enough for me to see the expression on his face, tears of joy flowed down my cheeks. I felt the kind of instant relief only someone under the absolute sentence of death feels when he receives an unlimited pardon. We rejoiced at the failures of the old king's project, and after staying at the spring through the night, we set out for home early in the morning.

🌿

SIX

No People Can Live More Happily

I was married to an Indian named Hiokatoo when my son Thomas was about four years old. Hiokatoo was six feet and four inches tall, large-boned, and quite lean. He was very active for a man of his size, and many said that Hiokatoo never found another Indian who could keep up with him in a race or throw him while wrestling. His eye was quick and his voice was powerful, the kind that demands attention. As a warrior, he was a terrifying foe. We had four daughters and two sons. I named my children after my deceased relatives, calling the girls Jane, Nancy, Betsey, and Polly, and the boys John and Jesse.

After the end of the French and Indian War in 1763, our tribe had nothing to trouble it until the beginning of the Revolutionary War in 1775. During those twelve years, the tomahawk and the scalping knife were not used, nor was the war-whoop heard, except on days of festivity. On these occasions, the achievements of former times were commemorated in dramas in which the chiefs and warriors re-enacted their skills in ambushing and killing ene-

False faces, or masks, were worn at a ceremony held at the end of the year to drive out evil spirits. These masks were carved from basswood trees or fashioned from corn husks. At this ceremony, the Senecas also made as much noise as possible, a practice similar to many modern-day American celebrations held on New's Year Eve, when noisemakers are very common. The American custom, started hundreds of years ago in Europe to drive out evil spirits there, is similar to one practiced in Asia for hundreds of years as well.

When a Seneca became ill, tribe members who had false faces were called in to drive out the evil spirit that had caused the illness. When the sick person recovered, he or she was expected to make a mask and help cure the next ill person in the tribe. Courtesy of Dover Pictorial Archive Series.

mies, thereby preserving and handing down to the children the theory of Indian warfare.

During this period, the Indians also observed the religious rites of their ancestors. The Indians followed customs with exactness and enthusiasm, and they offered sacrifices to the Great Good Spirit, whom they wor-

This picture by an Iroquois artist shows tribal members giving thanks to the Great Good Spirit. The Senecas believed that the Great Good Spirit was the creator of the world and of every good thing in it. They also believed that good Indians would be rewarded in the future in a place that would be perfect and pleasant.

The Senecas held five thanksgivings each year. They honored the Great Good Spirit after maple syrup had been gathered, after crops were planted, when kernels of corn began to appear on the cob, after corn was harvested, and at the end of the last moon. The last festival continued for nine days. During this time, the Senecas drove off evil spirits, made sacrifices to atone for their sins of the past year, smoked the peace pipe, and held banquets. Notice the use of the false face in the celebration pictured here. Courtesy of Dover Pictorial Archive Series.

shipped and adored for giving them, they believed, every good thing they enjoyed.

They also practiced various athletic activities, such as running, wrestling, leaping, and playing ball, to keep their bodies supple and their minds fit, so that they would be able to make the right decisions about ruling their nation or winning wars in the future.

No people can live more happily than Indians in times of peace before liquor was introduced to them. Their lives were a continual round of pleasures. Their wants were few and easily satisfied, and their cares were only for today, for they did not worry about the uncertainties of tomorrow. If peace ever dwelt with men, it was in former times during the breaks between wars amongst people now called barbarians. The moral character of the Indians was, if I may be allowed the expression, uncontaminated. Their fidelity was perfect. They were strictly honest, and they despised deception and falsehood. Chastity was held in high esteem, and a violation of it was considered sacrilege. They were temperate in their desires, moderate in their passions, and candid and honorable in the expression of their sentiments.

Shortly before the Revolutionary War began, the colonists sent for our leaders and the chiefs of the *Six Nations*. The colonists wanted to know which tribes would be their friends—or enemies!—in the coming war, which was then upon the point of breaking out between them and the King of England.

Our Indians attended a council at German Flats. The pipe of peace was smoked, and a treaty was made in which the Six Nations solemnly agreed that if a war should start, they would not take up arms on either side. With this, the colonists were satisfied, and they did not ask the Indians' assistance, nor did they wish it.

About a year later, a messenger arrived from the British commissioners, requesting all warriors of our tribe to attend a council at Oswego. At this council, the commissioners asked the Six Nations to help subdue the rebels, the colonists who had risen up against the good king, their master, and were about to rob him of his possessions and wealth. The chiefs then arose and told the commissioners of their treaty with the colonists, and they insisted that they would not violate it.

But the commissioners continued to plead for help. They told our people that the colonists were few in number and that they could easily be beaten, and, they said, the white men on account of their disobedience to the king merited all the punishment that was possible for the British and Indians to inflict upon them. The king, they added, was very rich, and his rum was as plentiful as the water in Lake Ontario. In addition, his men were as numerous as the sand upon the lake shore, which guaranteed success. If the Indians would assist in the war, the commissioners said, the Six Nations should never want for money or goods.

[Upon this statement, the chiefs of the Mohawks, Onandagas, Cayugas, and Senecas concluded a treaty with the king in which they agreed to take up arms against the rebels. The chiefs of the Oneidas and Tuscaroras sided with the colonists. Thus the Six Nations were divided.]

As soon as the treaty was finished, the commissioners gave presents to each Indian who agreed to support the British. Each one received a suit of clothes, a brass kettle, a gun, a tomahawk, a scalping knife, a quantity of powder and lead, a piece of gold, and a promise of a bounty for every scalp that was brought in. Thus richly clad and well equipped, they returned home after an absence of about two weeks, full of the fire of war and anxious to encounter their enemies. Many of the kettles that the Indians received at that time are now in use on the Genesee flats.

Hired to plunder and destroy the rebels, our warriors waited impatiently to begin their labor until sometime in the spring of 1776. At that time, some of our Indians were at Cau-tega, and they shot a man for the sole purpose of starting hostilities, as I was informed by my brother who was present.

In May, our Indians were in their first battle with the colonists. While they were absent, my daughter Nancy was born.

Later that year, our Indians took a woman and her three daughters prisoners at Cherry Valley and brought the woman to Little Beard's Town, where I now resided. They were eventually redeemed at Fort Niagara.

In the same expedition, Joseph Smith was taken prisoner and held until after the war ended. He was then liberated, and the Indians made him a present, along with Horatio Jones, another prisoner, of 6,000 acres of land lying in the present town of Leicester.

Just before the battle at Fort Stanwix, the British sent for the Indians to come and see them whip the rebels. The British said that they did not wish to have the Indians fight, just sit down, smoke their pipes, and look

Joseph Brant

Joseph Brant, born in 1742, was a Mohawk chief, who lived in what is now Upper New York State. He became one of the most highly respected and best known leaders of the Six Nations.

When Brant was only thirteen years old, he began to assist Sir William Johnson, who served as an Indian agent for the British crown in the Mohawk Valley. Johnson, whose duties included buying pelts from the Indians, was especially well received by the Iroquois, in large part because he genuinely cared about their well being. Brant accompanied Johnson on at least one military expedition against the French during the French and Indian War.

Johnson, whose common-law wife was Molly Brant, Joseph's

sister, was deeply impressed with Joseph's abilities both on and off the battlefield, and in 1761, when Joseph was nineteen, Johnson sent Brant to Eleazar Wheelock's Indian School in Lebanon, Connecticut. Here Joseph became a Christian. He joined the Anglican Church and was determined to become a missionary among his people.

But in 1763, Brant became a warrior again. Several Indian tribes refused to accept the terms of the peace treaty, in which they had no voice, that ended the French and Indian War, and they began a bloody revolt against the British who now claimed old French territory. When Brant received word of the uprising, he returned to the Mohawk Valley to help Johnson put down the rebellion.

Before war broke out between the colonists and Great Britain, Brant tried to persuade the Six Nations to support the British. He became a captain in the British Army in 1775, and he led the Iroquois who chose to support the king in battles against the rebels as well as in raids against the colonists on the frontier.

When Brant realized that the British would lose the war, he went to England to seek help for his people from the King of England. Brant and his followers were promised—and they received—a large parcel of land in Canada, where they could continue to live under British rule.

In Canada, Brant returned to his religious interests. He translated the Anglican Book of Common Prayer and the Gospel of Mark from the Bible into Mohawk.

Joseph Brant. Courtesy of The New York State Library, Manuscripts and Special Collections/Ann Aronson Photography.

on. All our warriors went, to a man, but instead of just watching, they were obliged to fight for their lives. At the end of the battle, they were completely beaten. Our Indians suffered great losses, thirty-six were killed, and a great number had been wounded. Our town was a scene of real sorrow and distress when the warriors returned and reported their misfortunes.

During the revolution, my house was the home of Colonels Walter Butler, a loyalist, and Joseph Brant whenever they chanced to come into our neighborhood as they passed to and from Fort Niagara, which was the seat of their military operations. Many a night, I have pounded samp for them from sunset until sunrise or furnished them with necessary provision and clean clothing for their journey.

❧

SEVEN

A Large and Powerful Army

For four or five years, we sustained no loss in war except for the few killed in distant battles, and our tribe, because of its remote location, felt secure from attack. But in the fall of 1779, we received word that a large and powerful army of rebels under the command of General John Sullivan was making rapid progress toward our settlement. Sullivan's men were destroying huts and cornfields, killing cattle, hogs, and horses, and cutting down orchards belonging to Indians throughout our country.

Our warriors immediately became alarmed, and they feared that Sullivan's men might take them by surprise and destroy everything in a single blow. To prevent so great a catastrophe, they sent out a few spies, who were to keep themselves at a short distance in front of the invading army in order to give information of its advances.

Sullivan arrived at Canandaigua Lake, which lay less than fifty miles east of us, and after he finished his work of destruction there, we learned that he was about to march to the Genesee River. Our warriors resolved to

Sullivan's Expedition

By early 1779, colonists on the frontier had made many requests for protection from the Indians. On February 25, 1779, the Continental Congress directed General George Washington to take action. Washington then ordered General John Sullivan to destroy Iroquois settlements and capture as many prisoners as possible to be held as hostages.

The first destruction took place at Chemung, a site close to a city now known as Elmira, New York. Here, one colonial major noted in his journal, "We had a glorious bonfire of upwards of thirty buildings at once." Another officer noted later as the men moved westward that almost everything edible was destroyed, including "acres of the best corn that ever I saw . . . and great quantities of beans, potatoes, pumpkins, cucumbers, squashes, and watermelons" as well as "fruit trees that appeared to be of great age." In one Indian village alone, more than 1,500 fruit trees were cut down.

Although Sullivan was successful in destroying forty villages, he was unable to capture many Indians. One exception occurred near Cayuga Lake where an old woman who was ill and a young boy who was crippled were not able to go into hiding. When the army found them, officers decided not to take the two hostages. Instead, the woman and boy were told to go into one of the houses, which was to be left for them. Shortly after the two entered the house, the doors were bolted on the outside, and the house was set on fire. The Indians were burned alive.

give him battle on the way and prevent, if possible, the horrors to which they knew we should be subjected if Sullivan reached our town. The men sent all the women and children into the woods a little west of Little Beard's Town so that we might make a retreat if it should become necessary to do so. Then well armed, the warriors set out to face the enemy. The place which they fixed upon for their battle lay between Honeoye Creek and the head of Conesus Lake, about thirty miles away.

At length, a scouting party from Sullivan's army arrived at the spot selected. The Indians then arose from their ambush with all the fierceness and terror that it was possible for them to exercise, and they forced the enemy to retreat.

Two Oneida Indians were taken prisoner in this skirmish. One of them was a guide for Sullivan, and this guide had provided the rebels with valuable information. At the beginning of the war, this Indian's brother had tried to persuade him to support the British, but he refused to do so. So the two brothers fought on opposite sides, and now they met, one as a prisoner, the other as a conqueror. The conqueror immediately recognized his brother, and approaching him with all the haughtiness of Indian pride heightened by a sense of power, he addressed him in the following manner:

"Brother, you have merited death! The hatchet or the war club will finish your career! When I begged you to follow me in the fortunes of war, you were deaf to my cries. Instead, when the rebels raised their weapons to fight their good king, you sharpened your knife and brightened your rifle and led our foes to our homelands. When those rebels forced us to seek new homes, it was you who dared to step forth as their guide and lead them to the doors of our new wigwams to butcher our children and put us to death! No crime can be greater! But though you have merited death and shall die on this spot, my hands shall not be stained by the blood of a brother." He then turned to the warriors around him. "Who will strike?"

Little Beard, who was standing by, immediately struck the prisoner on the head, killing him at once. Little Beard then informed the other Indian prisoner that as they were at war with the whites only, they would spare his life.

The Oneida warrior did not trust Little Beard, and he watched for a chance to make his escape, which he soon effected. Our Indians pursued him, and in doing so, fell in with a small detachment of Sullivan's men. The warriors had a short but severe skirmish in which they killed a number of the enemy and captured Captain William Boyd and a private.

The warriors took the prisoners to Little Beard's Town, where they were put Boyd to death in the most shocking manner. Little Beard, in this, as in all other scenes of cruelty that happened in this town, was the principal actor. Boyd was stripped of his clothing and tied to a small tree where the Indians threatened his life by throwing their tomahawks at the tree, directly over his head. Having punished him sufficiently in this way, they made a small opening in his abdomen and took out an end of his intestine and tied it to the tree. They untied Boyd and drove him around the tree until he had drawn out the whole of his intestines. He was then beheaded, and his head was stuck upon a pole. His body was left on the ground, unburied. The other prisoner was also beheaded.

This tragedy being finished, our Indians held a short council. After a long debate, they decided that they were not strong enough to drive Sullivan back, nor could they prevent him from taking possession of their fields. However, they believed it was possible to escape with their lives and to save their families. The women and children were then sent on towards Buffalo to a creek called Catawba. Some of the warriors accompanied the women while the remainder hid themselves in the woods behind Little Beard's Town to watch the movements of the army.

One or two days later, Sullivan and his men arrived at the Genesee River, where they destroyed every article of food that they could lay their hands on. They burned part of our corn and threw the rest into the river. They also burned our houses, killed what few cattle and horses they could find, destroyed our fruit trees, and left nothing but the bare soil. When we returned, there was not a mouthful of food left, not even enough to keep a child one day from perishing with hunger.

The weather by this time had become cold and stormy. I immediately resolved to take my children and look out for myself. I took two of my little ones on my back and told the other three to follow me. That night we arrived at Gardeau flats, where I have ever since resided.

At that time, two former slaves, who had run away from their Southern masters, were the only inhabitants of these flats. They lived in a small cabin, and they had raised a large field of corn, which they had not yet picked.

They were in need of help, and I worked for them, husking corn until the whole crop was harvested. I have laughed a thousand times to myself when I have thought of the good man who hired me and how he stood guard over me. He feared that I should get taken or injured by the Indians, and he stood by me constantly with a loaded gun in his hands in order to keep off the enemy while I husked his corn. By doing this, he lost as much labor of his own as he received from me.

However, I was not displeased with his attention, and I knew I would need all the corn that I could earn. I was allowed to keep every tenth string of husked corn for myself, and I earned one hundred strings of ears this way, which were equal to twenty-five bushels of shelled corn. This supply made many cakes and kept my family comfortably fed through the winter.

That winter was one of the most severe that I have ever witnessed. The snow fell about five feet deep, and the weather was extremely cold. Almost all the game upon which the Indians depended died from lack of food, their supply lying beneath the deep snow. This reduced the Indians almost to a state of starvation themselves through that winter and three or four succeeding years. Many of our people barely escaped with their lives, and some actually died from hunger and freezing.

Having been driven out of Little Beard's Town, I had no shelter and lacked the means of building one before winter set in, and my husband, who was at war, was unable to help me.

But after a short acquaintance with the former slaves, I found that they were kind and friendly, and at their request, my children and I took up residence with them in their cabin until I was able to provide a hut for myself. I lived more comfortably than I expected to through the winter, and in the spring I made a shelter near the cabin for myself and my family.

The two men continued to live on the flats two or three years after this, and then they left for a place that they expected would suit them much better. Although this land officially did not become mine until almost twenty years later when I was given a deed to it by the chiefs of the Six Nations [Council of Big Tree, 1797], I have lived on the flats from that time to the present, regarding the area as my own.

My flats had been cleared long ago. It was the opinion of the oldest Indians at Genishau that the land had been improved before any of the Indian tribes ever saw it. I well remember that soon after I went to Little Beard's Town, the banks of Fall Brook were washed off, and this exposed a large number of human bones. The Indians then said that these relics were not the bones of Indians, because they had never heard of any of their dead being buried there. They believed that the bones belonged to a race of *ancient people* who a great many moons before had cleared the land and lived on the flats.

The next summer, our Indians, enraged at the whites for the treatment they had received, decided to seek revenge by destroying some frontier settlements. Cornplanter led the warriors, and an officer by the name of Johnston commanded the British in the expedition. The force was large and so strongly bent upon revenge that seemingly nothing could avert its march nor prevent its depredations. After leaving the Genesee River, the men marched eastward to the source of the Susquehanna River, and then using a series of creeks and rivers, sailed as far east as Fort

Cornplanter, son of a Dutch trader from Albany, was a Seneca warrior. He was best known for his ability to control quick tempers in the men about him. Courtesy of the New York State Library, Manuscripts and Special Collections/Ann Aronson Photography.

Stanwix before starting home. On their route they burned a number of places, destroyed all the cattle and property that they came upon, killed many white people, and brought home a few prisoners.

Old John O'Bail was one of these prisoners. In his younger days, O'Bail had frequently passed through Indian settlements near Fort Niagara, and he had fallen in love with one of the squaws with whom he had a son who was called Cornplanter.

Cornplanter was a chief of considerable eminence, and he had been informed of his parentage. After he had taken his father, he stepped before him and said, "I am your son. You are now my prisoner and subject to the customs of Indian warfare, but you shall not be harmed, and you need not fear. I was eager to see you and to greet you in friendship. Indians love their friends and their kindred and treat them with kindness. If you choose to live with our people, I will cherish you and furnish you with plenty of venison, and your life will be easy. If it is your choice to return to your fields and live with your white children, I shall send a party of my trusty young men to conduct you back in safety. I respect you, my father. You have been friendly to Indians, and they are your friends."

John O'Bail chose to return. Cornplanter, as good as his word, ordered a party of young men to escort him, which they did with the greatest care.

Sometime near the close of the Revolutionary War, 1779 or '80, Ebenezer Allen, a *Tory* who had accompanied our warriors on raids against the colonists, left his people in Pennsylvania and came to the Genesee River to live with the Indians, who had now returned to the river to try to repair the damage Sullivan had done. Allen was without any business that would support him, but he soon became acquainted with my oldest son Thomas, who now was about eighteen years old, and the two men hunted together.

That spring, Allen worked my flats, and he continued to labor there until after the peace treaty was signed in 1783. He then went to Philadelphia on some business that detained him but a few days. He returned with a horse and some dry goods that he carried to a place called Mount Morris, which lies about ten miles north of my flats, where he decided to live.

Although peace had been declared by this time, the Indians on the Niagara frontier, especially Red Jacket, were dissatisfied with the terms of the treaty, and they were determined, at all hazards, to continue their attacks upon the white settlements that lay between them and Albany, including Mount Morris. They actually made ready and were about to set out on an expedition when Allen, who by this time understood our customs of war, stole a belt of wampum. He carried it as a token of peace from the Indians to the commander of the nearest American military post, where the belt was eagerly accepted. Upon learning what had happened, our warriors were chagrined and disappointed beyond measure, but as they held the wampum to be a sacred thing, they dared not go against its meaning. Shortly after, they smoked the pipe of peace.

However, they resolved to punish Allen for his meddling in their national affairs. A party was dispatched from Niagara to apprehend him and bring him in for a trial. But just before the party arrived, Allen got news of its approach, and he fled to safety. After many months of hiding from his enemies, some of which he spent at my house, Allen was turned in by some whites. He was taken to Montreal, Canada, for trial, where he was acquitted.

Shortly after, Allen returned to the Genesee River, where he planted corn and built a grist and saw mill on the falls, at a place now called Rochester.

Red Jacket was a powerful speaker and a well-known warrior. He objected strongly to the terms of the peace treaty because it took away so much land from the Senecas. Also, he didn't trust the colonists who he thought would seize even more land. As a result, Red Jacket wanted to continue to fight, an idea that Cornplanter rejected because he feared that the Senecas might lose everything if they did not accept the colonists' peace proposal. Courtesy of the New York State Library, Manuscripts and Special Collections/Ann Aronson Photography.

EIGHT

❦

Land That
I Could
Call My Own

After the peace treaty was signed in 1783 many white prisoners were being freed. About this time, my Indian brother, Black Coals, offered me my liberty. He told me that if I wanted to, I could go to my friends and take my five children from my marriage to Hiokatoo with me: John, sixteen years old; nine-year-old Nancy; six-year-old Betsey; five-year-old Polly and Jane, who was then an infant.

My son Thomas, now twenty years old, was eager that I should go, and he offered to go with me and assist me on the journey by taking care of the younger children and providing food as we traveled through the wilderness. But the chiefs of our tribe, suspecting from his appearance, actions, and a few warlike exploits that Thomas, son of Sheninjee, would be a great warrior or a good councilor, refused to let him leave them on any account whatever.

To go myself and leave him was more than I felt able to do, for he had been kind to me and was one on whom

I placed great dependence. But the chiefs refusal to let him go was only one reason for my resolving to stay; another more powerful reason, if possible, was the fact that I had a large family of Indian children that I must take with me, and if I should be so fortunate as to find my relatives, I feared that they would despise my children—and me—and treat us as enemies, or at least with a degree of cold indifference, which I thought I could not endure.

After I had duly considered the matter, I told my brother that it was my choice to stay and spend the remainder of my days with my Indian friends and live with my family as I had heretofore done. He appeared well pleased with my resolution and informed me that since that was my choice, I should have a piece of land that I could call my own, where I could live unmolested and have something at my death to leave for the benefit of my children.

Shortly after, he made himself ready to go to Canada with Joseph Brant. Before he left us, he said that he would speak to some of the chiefs at Buffalo who would attend the *Great Council,* which he expected would convene in a few years, and he would ask them to give me a tract of land that I selected. My brother left us, and soon after he died.

Black Coals was an excellent man, and he always treated me with kindness. Perhaps no one of his tribe at any time exceeded him in natural mildness of temper and warmth and tenderness of affection. If he had taken my life when the greedy old king had wanted to redeem me, Black Coals's action would have been done with a pure heart and from good motives. He loved his friends, and he was generally beloved. During the time that I lived in

The Senecas gave Mary Jemsion more than 17,000 acres. Part of her land and the Genesee River are pictured here. Courtesy of Letchworth State Park, Castile, New York.

the family with him, he never offered the most trifling abuse. On the contrary, his whole conduct towards me was strictly honorable. I mourned the loss of a tender brother, and I shall remember him with emotions of friendship and gratitude.

I lived undisturbed, without hearing a word on the subject of my land until the Great Council was finally held in 1797. Farmer's Brother, an Indian, sent for me. When I arrived in Buffalo, Farmer's Brother told me that my brother had spoken to him about reserving a piece of land for my use, and now it was time for me to receive it. He asked me to choose a tract that would suit me and describe its boundaries. I told him the place of beginning and then went around the tract that I judged would be sufficient for my purpose, knowing that it would include the Gardeau flats.

When the council opened, Farmer's Brother presented my claim. Red Jacket opposed me with all his influence since he did not want to surrender any Seneca soil. However, Farmer's Brother insisted that I have land upon which to live with my children, and he won over the council. The deed was made and signed, giving to me the title to all the land I had described, placing it under the same restrictions and regulations that governed other Indian lands. That land, more than 17,000 acres, has ever since been known as the Gardeau Tract.

About 300 acres of my land was flat land that lay near the Genesee River. It was supposed that these flats had been cleared by an ancient people that I mentioned before. The land was extremely fertile, but needed more labor than my daughters and I were able to perform to produce enough grain and other produce to feed us. The land had been uncultivated for so long that it was thickly covered with weeds of almost every description. In order that we might live more easily, I was given permission by the chiefs to lease my land to white people to work on shares. I have continued to lease land, and the income it brings supports me in comfort.

In late 1809 or early 1810 Captain Horatio Jones, a former Seneca captive, told me that a cousin of mine, George Jemison, was living in Leicester, a few miles from Gardeau. George Jemison, Jones said, was very poor, and he thought that I should go see him and take him home to live on my land. My Indian friends were pleased to hear that one of my relatives was so near, and they also advised me to send for him and his family immediately. I then had him and his family moved into one of my houses in March 1810.

George said that he was my father's brother's son and that his father did not leave Europe until after the French and Indian War in America had ended. He said that his father settled in Pennsylvania, where he died. George had no personal knowledge of my father, but from information he had been given, he was confident that we were cousins. Although I had never heard my father speak of more than one brother, and he died long ago, I knew that is was possible that he might have had another brother, and I received George as a kinsman and treated him with every degree of friendship that his situation demanded.

He was destitute and in debt to the amount of seventy dollars without the ability to pay one cent. I paid his debts and bought him a cow, for which I paid twenty dollars. I also purchased a sow with young pigs for eight dollars, as well as other provisions and furniture so that his family was comfortable. Since he had no team of oxen, I furnished him with one and supplied him with tools for farming as well as loaning him some of Thomas's cows for two seasons. My only object in mentioning his poverty and the articles I supplied is to show how ungrateful a person can be for favors and how soon a benefactor can be forgotten.

Thus furnished with the necessary tools for farming, a good team and as much land as he could till, George began farming on my flats, and for a while he worked hard. At length, however, he got the idea that if he could become owner of a part of my tract, he could live more easily and become wealthy besides. So he set up a plan to obtain the land in the easiest manner possible.

After I had supported him for some six or seven years, a friend of mine told me that since Jemison was my cousin and very poor, I ought to give him a piece of land so that he might have something that he could call his own. My friend and Jemison then came to my house, prepared to complete a bargain. I asked how much land he wanted. Jemison said that he should be glad to receive his old field, as he called it, containing about fourteen acres, and another one that contained twenty-six.

I told them that I was incapable of making such a business deal on my own, and I wanted to wait until Thomas Clute, a neighbor on whom I depended for advice, returned from a trip before doing anything about giving away land. To this, Jemison replied that if I waited until Mr. Clute returned, he should not get the land at all, and he appeared very eager to have the business closed without delay. I was inclined to give him some land, but since I could not read, I feared to do it alone, lest he include as much land as he pleased without my knowledge.

He then read the deed that my friend had prepared, describing a piece of land by certain bounds that were a specified number of *chains and links* from each other. Not understanding the length of a chain or link, I described the bounds of a piece of land that I intended Jemison should have, which he said was just the same as the deed contained. Putting confidence in him, I signed the deed to George Jemison, conveying to him, I thought, forty acres of land. When the deed was completed he told me never to mention the bargain that I had made to any person. If I did, he said, it would break the contract.

The deal was disclosed later anyway, and it was then that I learned that the deed, instead of containing forty acres, contained four hundred. One half of this was given to my friend by Jemison as a reward for his trouble in making out the deed. My friend, however, upon the advice of some powerful people, eventually gave up his claim.

As soon as I found out my cousin's true disposition, I got him off my premises as quickly as possible. I also sent Thomas's son to Jemison to take back a cow that I had just recently let him use. Jemison refused to let her go, and he struck my grandson so violently with a club, the blow almost killed him. Jemison then tried to have the boy arrested on some trumped up charge so he wouldn't return for the cow again. But Young King, our Indian chief, went to the white men's authorities, and he explained what really had happened. Jemison had to promise never to use his club again. Eventually he sold his land for a trifle to a gentleman in the southern part of Genesee County.

✿

NINE

My Troubles
Were Renewed

I have frequently heard it said by white people, and can truly say from my own experience, that the time in which parents take the most satisfaction and comfort from their families is when their children are young. Few mothers have had less trouble with their young children than I. My children were friendly to each other, and it was very seldom that I knew them to have the least difference or quarrel.

My happiness in this respect, however, was not without limits. My son Thomas, from the time he was a small lad and for some cause unknown to me, always called his brother John a witch. This was the cause, as they grew towards manhood, of frequent and severe quarrels between them, and the arguments caused me much anxiety for their safety.

After Thomas and John reached manhood, John took two wives with whom he lived until the time of his death. Although having more than one wife at a time was tolerated in our tribe, Thomas considered this practice

The Senecas, like many colonists, believed in witches. This Iroquois drawing pictures Atotarho (seated), a mythical Seneca figure so mean and cunning he was thought to be a witch. Notice the snakes in his hair.

People accused of witchcraft often had unusual strength or abilities. Men and women who showed a great ability to cure the sick, for example, were thought to have supernatural power. How else, everyone wondered, could anyone explain such success? Courtesy of Dover Pictorial Archive Series.

wrong. Consequently, he often scolded John, telling him that his conduct was beneath the dignity of a gentleman, indecent, and inconsistent with the principles of good Indians. John deeply resented being lectured by his brother.

However, my sons never actually quarreled unless Thomas was intoxicated. In his fits of drunkenness, Thomas seemed to lose all his natural reason, and he conducted himself like a wild man. At such times, he often threatened to take my life for having raised a witch, and he has gone so far as to raise his tomahawk to split my head. He, however, never struck me, but he did strike Hiokatoo, and this excited great indignation in John.

No one can conceive of the constant trouble that I daily endured on account of my two oldest sons, whom I loved equally and with all the feelings and affection of a tender mother. Parents, mothers especially, will love their children even though they may be ever so unkind and disobedient. Even when the children have committed the greatest wrong, a parent's love will be strengthened to reach and reclaim the wanderer.

But despite my efforts to help my sons get along with each other, year after year, their hatred for each other increased. Then on the fateful day of July 1, 1811, while I was away, Thomas, after having several drinks, came to my house, where he found John. Thomas immediately began a quarrel, and John's anger flared. John caught Thomas by his hair, dragged him out the door and killed him with his tomahawk!

I returned soon after and found my son lifeless at the door. No one can judge my feelings on seeing this mournful spectacle, and what added greatly to my distress was the fact that he had fallen by the murderous hand of his brother! I felt my situation unbearable. Now nearly seventy years old and having passed through many scenes of trouble of the most cruel and trying kind, I had hoped to spend my few remaining days in tranquillity and to die in peace, surrounded by my family. This fatal event, however, seemed to blast all my prospects.

Some of my neighbors came in to assist me in taking care of the corpse and to console me the best they could. Thomas was buried in a style corresponding with his rank.

He, except when intoxicated, which was not often, was a kind and tender child, willing to assist me in my labor and to remove every obstacle to my comfort. His natural abilities were said to be of a superior cast, and he soared above the trifling subjects of revenge, which are common among Indians. In his childhood days, he loved to practice the art of war, though he despised the cruelties that the warriors inflicted upon their prisoners. He was a great councilor and chief when he was quite young.

At the time he was killed, Thomas was fifty-two years old, and John was forty-eight. Thomas would not have come to so untimely an end if it hadn't been for his intemperance. He fell victim to the use of liquor, a poison that will soon exterminate the Indian tribes in this part of the country.

As soon as I had recovered a little from this heart-breaking event, I hired an Indian named Shanks to go to Buffalo and carry the sorrowful news of Thomas's death to our friends there and to ask the chiefs to hold a council to deal with John as they thought proper. John, fearing that he would be apprehended and punished, went into hiding.

The chiefs soon assembled in council, and after examining the matter according to their laws, the council acquitted John. They felt that Thomas had started the fight, and they believed that he deserved the treatment he had received from his brother. John, upon learning the decision of the council, returned to his family.

On November 1811, only a few months after Thomas's death, my husband died at the advanced age of 103 years, as nearly as his years could be estimated. He had been suffering from *consumption* for four years. Hiokatoo was my last connection to my old friends and family members. Now all had passed away, except a part of one family, which now lives at Tonawanda near Buffalo.

Hiokatoo was buried decently, and he had all the items of a veteran warrior buried with him: a war club, a tomahawk, a scalping knife, a powder flask, pieces of flint and *spunk*, a small cake, and a cup. He was laid out in his best clothing.

I have frequently heard him repeat the history of his life, and when he came to the part that related his actions, his bravery, and his valor in war, his nerves seemed strung with youthful ardor, and the warmth of the able warrior seemed to animate his frame. Although war was his trade from youth and his cruelties to his enemies were unparalleled, he was a man of tender feelings to his friends, ready and willing to assist them in distress. During the nearly fifty years that I lived with him, I received, according to Indian customs, all the kindness and attention that was my due as his wife. His health had been consistently good until his last years.

Being left a widow in my old age to mourn the loss of a husband with whom I had six children and having suffered the loss of a son, I hoped that I would be spared further tragedy. But a short time later, my troubles were renewed.

My son Jesse went to Mount Morris on business in the winter after his father died. John, who happened to be at Mount Morris then, met Jesse there and invited him to travel home together when Jesse's business was finished. Jesse, fearing that John would start a fight, declined the invitation. From that time on, John thought that Jesse despised him, and he was enraged at the treat-

Hiokatoo

[James Seaver included a biographical sketch of Hiokatoo in Mary's narrative. Seaver got his information from George Jemison, the man who claimed he was Mary's cousin. The following is a shortened version of the original sketch.]

In early life, Hiokatoo attended only to the art of war. He regularly practiced using his tomahawk and scalping knife, and he inflicted cruelties upon animals that chanced to fall into his hands. In that way, he learned to use his implements of war effectively, and at the same time, he blunted all those fine feelings and sympathies that are aroused by seeing a fellow being in distress. Eventually he could inflict the most awful tortures upon his enemies, and he prided himself upon his fortitude in having performed such tortures without the least degree of pity or remorse.

In 1731, he was made a runner, and he assisted in collecting an army to go against the Cotawpes, Cherokees, and other southern Indians. The battle continued for two days and two nights with the utmost severity, and the Northern Indians so far succeeded in destroying the Cotawpes that they ceased to be a nation.

In one battle, Hiokatoo captured a number of Indians whom he killed by tying them to trees and ordering boys to shoot arrows at them until death finished the misery of the sufferers. This process took two days for its completion!

During the French War he was in every battle fought on the Susquehanna and Ohio rivers. Following Braddock's defeat, he took two white prisoners at Fort Duquesne and burnt them alive in a fire of his own kindling.

In the Revolutionary War, he participated in the battle at Fort Freeland in Pennsylvania. The force that went against it consisted of 100 British regulars and 300 Indians under Hiokatoo. After a short, but bloody engagement, the fort was surrendered. The women and children were sent under an escort to the next fort, and the men and boys were taken off by a party of British soldiers to the Indians' encampment. As soon as the fort had surrendered, Hiokatoo, with the help of a few Indians, tomahawked every wounded American while they begged for mercy.

Hiokatoo also participated in an expedition that went out against Cherry Valley. Captain David, a Mohawk Indian, was first in command, and Hiokatoo was second. The force consisted of several hundred Indians, who were determined on mischief and the destruction of the whites.

Hiokatoo was in seventeen campaigns during the Revolutionary War, four of which were in the war with his old enemies, the Cherokee Indians. They had been weakened by attacks by the colonists, and Hiokatoo was so fully determined upon the Cherokees' destruction that he raised his own army. In one of these campaigns, which lasted two years, he drove the Cherokees out of their country and into the Creek Indian nation.

When he tired of war, he returned to his family. Towards the end of the war against the Cherokees, he took two squaws, whom he sold on his way home for money to defray the expense of his journey. He brought home a great number of scalps, which he had taken.

ment that he had received. Very little was said, however, for months.

Sometime in May 1812, Robert Whaley, who lived in Castile, within four miles of me, came to my house. He wanted to hire John, Jesse, and George Chongo, who was married to my daughter Polly, to help him slide boards from the top of the hill to the river, where he planned to build a raft of them for market. They all agreed to go with Mr. Whaley, and before they set out, I charged them not to drink any whiskey, for I was confident that if they did, they surely would have a quarrel as a result of drunkenness.

They worked until almost nightfall, when a quarrel took place between George and Jesse. Both of them had been drinking despite my warning, and their quarrel ended in a battle in which George got whipped. When Jesse was through with George, he told Mr. Whaley that he would go home. Jesse, however, went but a few rods before he stopped to lie down.

John, with a knife in his hand, went to Mr. Whaley as soon as Jesse was gone, and he told Whaley to be off. Mr. Whaley, seeing that John was determined upon something desperate, was alarmed for his own safety. By this time, Jesse was advancing towards John, trying to take away his knife. While they struggled, they fell, and John gave Jesse a fatal stab. John repeated the blows until Jesse cried out, "Brother, you have killed me!" and quit his hold on John and settled back upon the ground.

Upon hearing this, John left Jesse and went to Thomas's widow's house. Here he told the children that he had been fighting with their uncle, whom he had killed. He then showed them his knife.

The next morning, as soon as it was light, some of my grandchildren came to me and told me that Jesse was dead. They also informed me how he came by his death. John soon followed them, and he informed me himself of all that had taken place between him and his brother, and he seemed to be somewhat sorrowful for his conduct.

I went to the site of Jesse's death, and I was overcome with grief when I saw my murdered son. I lost command of myself, becoming so frantic, those who were present were obliged to hold me from going near him.

Jesse had received eighteen wounds so deep and large, it was believed by all who saw him that any of the wounds would have proved fatal. The corpse was carried to my house and kept for four days, when it was buried after the manner of burying white people.

Jesse was twenty-seven or twenty-eight years old when he was killed. He was naturally mild tempered and friendly. He was also inclined to copy after the white people, both in his manners and dress. He was well-acquainted with white people in the area, and he learned their work habits, which he was fond of practicing, especially when my comfort demanded his labor. As I have said, it is the custom among the Indians for women to perform all the labor in and out of doors, and I had the whole to do with the help of my daughters, until Jesse was old enough to help us. He worked in the cornfield, chopped my wood, milked my cows and worked at any task that would make my workload lighter. Since his death, I have had to do all my labor alone, and this has been difficult for me.

Because he was my youngest child and so willing to help me, I know that I loved him better than I did either of my other sons. Jesse shunned the company of his brothers and the Indians generally, and he never attended their ceremonies. This, together with my partiality for him, were probably the cause which raised so much envy in John, a degree of which nothing short of death could satisfy.

In April or May 1817, John, who was well-known among the Indians of various tribes for his skill in curing diseases with roots and herbs, was called upon to go to Buffalo and two other settlements to treat a number of patients. He was absent about two months.

When he returned, he saw the results of the *Great Slide* on the Genesee River, which had taken place while he was gone. For some reason, he considered the slide a sign of his coming death. He wept as he confided his fears to his sister, and although Nancy tried to persuade him that his trouble was imaginary, she was not able to end his mental sufferings.

Shortly after, John went to Squawky Hill, where he met two Squawky Hill Indians, Jack and Doctor. All three drank freely, and in the afternoon they had a bitter quarrel during which Jack and Doctor decided to kill John. After the quarrel ended, everyone appeared to be friendly, and John bought some more liquor, which all of them drank.

That night, the three of them set out for home. John was on horseback and the other two were on foot. They hadn't gone far when Jack and Doctor began another quarrel with John, grabbed him, dragged him off his horse, and gave him so severe a blow with a rock that some of his brains flew out of his head. John recovered a

me as a man of honesty and integrity, I sent for my son John for advice. He objected to my going into any bargain with Mr. Brooks without the consent of Mr. Clute. Mr. Brooks then repeated his statements for my advisor, and after Mr. Clute had consulted with others, he agreed that I should accept Brooks's help.

On April 19, 1817, an act was passed that made me a citizen of the United States and confirmed my title to my land. However, I could not sell my tract without the consent of the Seneca chiefs and Major Carrol, who had been appointed by the government to oversee any sale. I then leased 7,000 acres to Brooks until the land could be transferred to him. I also asked Mr. Clute to select a lot on the west side of my tract to compensate him for all his trouble.

By the winter of 1822–23, Brooks's acres still had not been officially turned over to him because the Seneca chiefs and the government had not granted permission for the sale to take place. Now I wished to sell the rest of my land with the exception of a tract, two miles long and one mile wide, near the river where I would live, and I asked Brooks to arrange a special hearing to do so.

On September 3 or 4, 1823, the hearing finally took place. At this meeting were Major Carrol, Judge Howell, N. Gorham, who represented the government, and upwards of twenty chiefs of our nation. Jasper Parrish, now an Indian agent, and Horatio Jones, an interpreter, were also present. The sale was agreed to unanimously, and I gave a deed to Brooks. In exchange for the land, Brooks has agreed to pay me, or my heirs, three hundred dollars a year forever. Whenever the land I kept is sold, the in-

Horatio Jones and Jasper Parrish

A number of white prisoners were held by the Senecas during the Revolutionary War, including Horatio Jones, whom Mary previously mentioned in Chapters 6 and 8, and Jasper Parrish.

Jones, a soldier, was captured toward the end of the war, and he was held in high esteem by the Senecas. Jones was given a chance to save his life by running the gauntlet. The warriors did their best to stop him by swinging clubs and throwing stones at the prisoner, but Jones managed to dodge most of the weapons, and he made it through the gauntlet without receiving many blows. He showed a great deal of spunk, which the Senecas admired, and as a captive, he refused to be intimidated. When one Indian threw a tomahawk at Jones to frighten him, Jones picked it up and threw it back, barely missing the Indian's head. On another occasion, Jones stuffed a hot squash down the shirt of an Indian who refused to stop teasing him.

Jasper Parrish was captured when he was eleven years old by a party of Delaware Indians. Parrish was passed from one tribe to another, reaching the Senecas toward the end of the war. He learned five or six dialects while he was a captive, and like Jones, he was well liked by the Senecas.

At the end of the war, Jones and Parrish were given their freedom, a requirement of the peace treaty. They decided to remain with the Indians, and the former prisoners received generous gifts of land from the Senecas. Jones and Parrish served as interpreters of Indian languages for the U.S. government.

come from the sale is to be equally divided amongst the members of the Seneca nation.

When I review my life, the privations that I have suffered, and the hardships that I have endured, it is a miracle that my reason and health have been spared. It has been a life filled with tragic events that I hope no one else will have to endure.

No one can pass from a state of freedom to that of slavery and be contented. The recollection of what we once had, our friends, our home, and the pleasures we enjoyed, remind us of our losses. The fear of a future filled with misery and wretchedness over which we have little control and the desire for freedom make slavery bitter. But bitterness can weaken the body, and we ought, when enslaved, to make every effort to accept our situation and do what we can to make it as bearable as possible.

For my long, healthy life, I am indebted to an excellent constitution with which I have been blessed. Also, the care of my own health was one of my principal concerns. By avoiding exposures to wet and cold and eating moderately, I have lived longer than I expected. I have never once been sick, only as I have mentioned, until this last year.

Spirits and tobacco I have never used, and I have never once attended an Indian *frolic*. When I was taken prisoner, and for sometime after that, liquor was not known, and when it was first introduced, it was in small quantities and used only by the warriors. Therefore, it was a long time before the women began to even taste it.

After the French War, for a number of years, it was

the practice of the warriors of our tribe to send to Niagara and get two or three kegs of rum, in all six or eight gallons, and hold a frolic for as long as the rum lasted. When it was brought to the town, all the warriors met, and before a drop was drunk, they gave all their knives, tomahawks, guns, and other instruments of war to one Indian, whose business it was to conceal the weapons and remain perfectly sober until the frolic ended.

Having thus divested themselves, the warriors began drinking, and they continued their frolic until every drop was consumed. If any of them became quarrelsome or began to fight, those who were sober enough bound them and laid them on the ground, where they were obliged to remain until they got sober, at which time they were untied. When the fumes of the liquor left the company, the sober Indian returned to each man the instruments with which he had entrusted him, and all went home satisfied. A frolic of that kind was held but once a year, when the Indians had finished their hunting season.

After the Revolutionary War, alcohol became common in our tribe, and liquor was frequently used by both sexes. Drinking has destroyed some of our people. I attribute my sons' deaths to drinking, and I believe that alcohol will bring about the extinction of our people.

My strength has been great for a woman of my size. After my captivity, I learned to carry loads in a pack on my back, with a strap placed across my forehead. These loads were often very heavy. Thirty years ago, with the help of my young children, I carried all the boards that were used in building my house from a mill five miles away. I have planted, hoed, and harvested corn every season but one since I was taken prisoner. Even this present

This is Nancy's house, which stood about eighty rods south of Mary's home. It is very similar in appearance to the description Mary gave of her own house, a timber building with a covered porch and shingled roof. Courtesy of Letchworth State Park, Castile, New York.

fall (1823), I have husked my corn and carried it on my back into my house.

I have never suffered for provisions since I came upon the flats. I have never been in debt to anyone, either, for the plenty that I have shared.

My vices have been few. It was believed for a long time, by some of our people, that I was a great witch. But they were unable to prove my guilt, and I escaped the doom of those who are convicted of witchcraft, a crime Indians consider as awful as murder.

I have been the mother of eight children. Three sons died as I have related, and my daughter Jane died more than thirty years ago. Three daughters have survived to this day. I live in my own house with my youngest daughter, Polly, who is married to George Chongo. They have three children. My daughter Nancy, who is married to Billy Green, lives about eighty rods south of my house, and she has seven children. My other daughter, Betsey, is married to John Green. She has seven children and resides eighty rods north of my house. I have thirty-nine grandchildren and fourteen great-grandchildren, all living in the neighborhood of the Genesee River or at Buffalo.

Thus situated in the midst of my children, I expect I shall soon leave the world and make room for the rising generation. I feel the weight of years with which I am loaded, and I am aware of my failing sight, hearing, and strength. But my only anxiety is for my family. If my heirs will live happily, I feel as though I could lay down in peace a life that has been filled with more troubles than are experienced by most mortals.

Afterword

Mary Jemison eventually sold all of her land and moved to an Indian reservation near Buffalo, New York. She died on the reservation in 1833, and she was buried in a cemetery near Buffalo.

In 1877, William Pryor Letchworth, a wealthy industrialist, began to buy up land along the Genesee River, including land Mary once owned. He was deeply impressed with the stories he heard about Mary, and he made a commitment to keep her story alive. First, Letchworth arranged to have Mary's remains removed from the cemetery in Buffalo and buried on land that was once hers. Then he commissioned Henry K. Bush-Brown to make a bronze statue of Mary to mark her grave. Letchworth also preserved Nancy's house and an old council house then set out to gather as much information about Jemison as he could. He willed his collections, buildings, and land to the state of New York for a park. His work has been carefully maintained, and today, visitors may stop at Mary's grave and tour the Letchworth Museum to learn more about this famous Indian captive.

Glossary

Ancient people. Algonquin or possibly Eskimo-like people. Historians believe that Algonquin Indians lived in this area for at least 5,000 years, long before the Senecas moved in. From time to time, Eskimo-like people attempted to take part of the area from the Algonquins. Which people were buried at Fall Brook is not certain.

Block and pestle. Tools used for grinding corn. The kernels were placed on a hard, flat surface, the block, and crushed with a hand-held tool with a wide surface at one end, the pestle.

Cake. A thin, flat bread made from corn meal.

Catechism. The principal religious beliefs of Christians, including the Ten Commandments. During Mary's time, parents often instructed their children in religion, and children were expected to memorize the catechism and to be able to recite portions when asked to do so.

Chains and links. Used to measure land. A link is 7.92 inches long. Each chain has 100 links, or sixty-six feet.

Consumption. A disease that causes the body to waste away. This term is usually used to refer to tuberculosis of the lungs.

Flaxseed. Produces flax, a plant that is highly valued for both its seed, which contains linseed oil, and its long stems, which are used to make linen, a durable fabric.

Frolic. A party. Unlike celebrations meant to honor someone or something, a frolic was held just for fun.

Genesee flats. The level land that bordered the Genesee River. It was ideal agricultural land, loose, rich, and close to a water supply if irrigation was needed.

Great Council. A meeting among the councilors elected from each of the Six Nations in the Iroquois League. These councilors were elected by women in each tribe. The council met for a variety of reason: to solve problems between the nations or to decide whether or not to declare war, for example.

Great Slide. A landslide. This slide occurred in May 1817, on the upper end of the Gardeau flats, when a large area near the Genesee River suddenly gave way. The slide covered more than twenty acres, changing the route of the river.

Hominy. A white corn that is crushed or coarsely ground and boiled in water or milk before being eaten.

Moon. A lunar month. The Indians used the moon to measure a period of time, approximately twenty-nine days. A new moon began when a slender crescent appeared. Twelve moons equaled a year. Many ancient civilizations used this system for telling time.

Provision. Supplies, usually foodstuffs.

Rod. A measurement equal to sixteen and one-half feet.

Running of the gauntlet. A test of courage and strength. Two long lines of Indians, about ten feet apart, faced each other and swung clubs or threw items at prisoners forced to run the length of the line between them. Prisoners who completed the gauntlet were thought to be unusually strong and brave, and they were allowed to live.

Samp. Coarse corn meal.

Shares. A system in which tenants work land in exchange for a portion of the crop.

Six Nations. Six Indians nations—Oneida, Seneca, Tuscarora, Mohawk, Onondaga, and Cayaga—which united and formed a government. These nations were known as the Iroquois League.

Spunk. A kind of wood or fungus used to start a fire.

Tory. Another name for a loyalist, a colonist who supported the British during the American Revolution.

Bibliography

Drimmer, Frederick, ed. Introduction to *Captured by the Indians: 15 Firsthand Accounts, 1750–1870*. New York: Dover Publications, 1961.

Grosvenor, Gilbert M., ed. *The World of the American Indian*. Washington, DC: National Geographic Book Service, 1974.

Halsey, Francis Whiting. *The Old New York Frontier*. New York: Charles Scribner's Sons, 1901.

McCall, Barbara A. *Indian Tribes of America: The Iroquois*. Vero Beach, Florida: Rourke Publications, 1989.

Namias, June, ed. Introduction to *A Narrative of the Life of Mrs. Mary Jemison* by James E. Seaver. Norman, Oklahoma: University of Oklahoma Press, 1992.

Parker, Arthur C. *The History of the Seneca Indians*. Port Washington, New York: Ira J. Friedman, 1926.

Ward, Christopher. *The War of the Revolution*. Vol. 2. New York: Macmillan Company, 1952.

For More Information

Boardman, Fon W., Jr. *Against the Iroquois: The Sullivan Campaign of 1779*. New York: David McKay Co., 1978. This book gives a detailed account of the Continental Army's attacks on the Indian tribes that supported the British.

Dickinson, Alice. *Taken by the Indians*. New York: Franklin Watts, 1976. Dickinson tells the stories of three men and three women (Mary Jemison is included) who were captured by Indians between 1676 and 1864. Portions of the captives' original accounts are included in each story.

Drimmer, Frederick, ed. *Captured by the Indians: 15 Firsthand Accounts, 1750–1870*. New York: Dover Publications, 1961. Meant for adult readers, younger readers may not want to tackle some of the vocabulary in this text. Those who decide to do so, however, will find some fascinating stories about white captives.

McCall, Barbara A. *The Iroquois*. Vero Beach, Florida: Rourke Publications, 1989. McCall discusses how the various tribes in the Iroquois confederacy, including the Senecas, lived. She examines festivals, rituals, games, religious beliefs, and everyday life in detail.

Molloy, Anne. *Wampum*. New York: Hastings House, 1977. Molloy explains how wampum was made, how the practice of using wampum got started, and how the practice spread from tribe to tribe. Molloy also explains what some of the most famous wampum belts mean in this heavily illustrated book.